D0170047

Getting underway

Getting underway

An explanation of how to sail a boat

Bud Tritschler

IM

INTERNATIONAL MARINE PUBLISHING CO.

Camden, Maine 04843

© 1987 by Highmark Publishing, Ltd.

All rights reserved. Except for use in a review, no part of this book may be reproduced or utilized in any form or by any means, electronic or mechanical, including photocopying, recording, or by any information storage and retrieval system, without written permission from the publisher.

Published by International Marine Publishing, a division of Highmark Publishing Ltd., 21 Elm Street, Camden, Maine 04843

Typeset by Camden Type 'n Graphics, Camden, Maine.
Text printed by BookCrafters, Chelsea, Michigan.
Covers printed by Rae Publishing Company, Cedar Grove, New Jersey.
Binding by A. Horowitz and Sons, Fairfield, New Jersey.

10 9 8 7 6 5 4 3 2 1

Library of Congress Number 87-2917
ISBN Number 0-87742-238-9

Dedicated to the memory of John T. Hayward
and his beautiful *Winifred*

Contents

PREFACE

In the course of assisting many people to absorb the rudiments of sailing, I have time and again sought to convey, without distortion, the essentials as they appear to me, rejecting versions and approaches that seemed to work less well than others. This book is a complete, step-by-step exposition of the teaching approaches I found most effective, from person to person, over the years. No one has heard it from beginning to end. No one ever needed to. Take from it what you need.

Sailing is easy to learn, requiring no extraordinary physical or mental accomplishments and only a little patience. It is easier still for some than for others. Like walking or bicycling, sailing teaches itself to those whose perceptions of reality are approximately normal.

Expert assistance in the earliest stages, however, accelerates learning by eliminating counterproductive ideas and behavior, concentrating on weak points, and helping the learner to generalize accurately about the experience as it happens. Comprehensible, workable generalization is the most valuable gift a teacher can offer, and that is what this little manual attempts.

Helping eager novices to begin properly has been one of my great pleasures. But of course, sailing isn't for everyone.

The personal dimensions of many simply do not include this area, a fact that is difficult for many sailors to accept. Let the avid mariner participate in a morning of skydiving, an afternoon of lawn bowls or poetry reading, a night at the dog track, ballroom dancing, or a spiritual revival, and he may admit to inadequate dimensions, too. None of us contains everything.

Should you sail? If intuition has not already replied, then a fair trial may be in order. In a sense, all acts are trials. Half a day, or even half an hour can settle the matter for some. One of my acquaintances owned and intemperately raced a variety of vessels, gaining, in the course of nearly ten years, a local reputation as a fine sailor before deciding against further trial. He had squeezed the fruit of all the juice he could pleasurably taste. My prize for gluttony goes to the famous French singlehander who, in recent times, rounded Cape Horn, almost certainly the winner of a nonstop round-the-world race if only he would hold for England and the finish line. Realizing that such a course would, in only about two months, bring an untimely end to the rapture of that particularly glorious cruise, he carried on another three-quarters of the globe to a more suitable destination. With unlimited stores, he might be sailing still.

If you should sail for a while, what will be your pleasure? Here is a catalog of possible reasons: To find unity with, or try oneself against, nature; to compete against others; to relieve, or experience and overcome, tension, fear, or anxiety; to improve or learn about self; to feed romantic fancy, change pace, sense freedom, relax; to create togetherness or be alone; to consume conspicuously; to become popular, to dominate others; to live on the water; to visit distant shores; to escape problems; to seek uncertainty. There must be many others.

Whatever your needs or desires, it is possible that sailing around in a boat may offer satisfaction. To find out, you must begin.

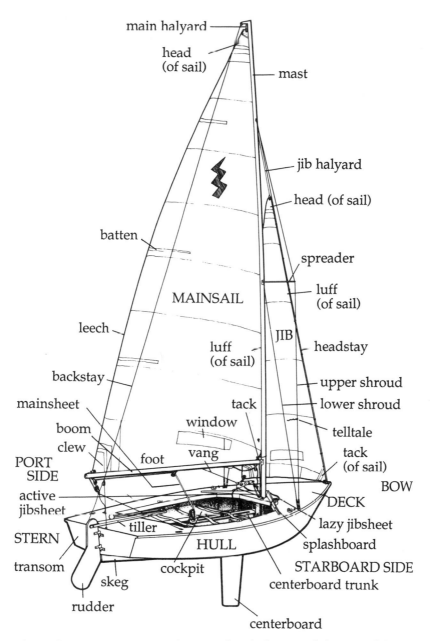

main halyard

head (of sail)

mast

jib halyard

head (of sail)

batten

spreader

luff (of sail)

MAINSAIL

JIB

leech

luff (of sail)

headstay

backstay

upper shroud

mainsheet

tack

lower shroud

boom

window

telltale

clew

foot

vang

tack (of sail)

PORT SIDE

BOW

active jibsheet

DECK

STERN

tiller

lazy jibsheet

splashboard

transom

HULL

STARBOARD SIDE

skeg

cockpit

centerboard trunk

rudder

centerboard

The Lightning, a centerboard boat raced actively around the United States and Canada since 1938.

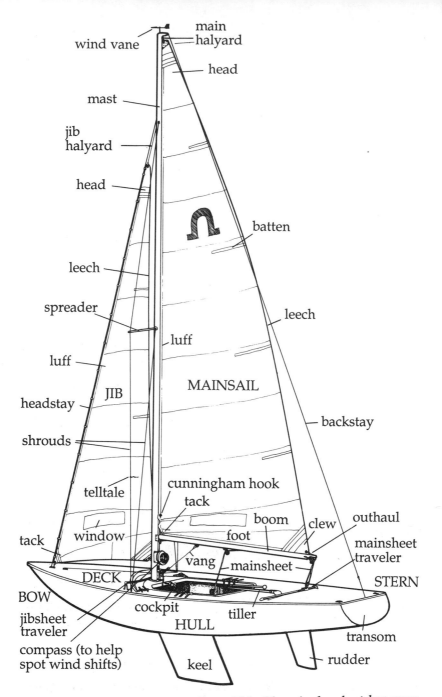

wind vane

main
halyard

head

mast

jib
halyard

head

batten

leech

spreader

luff

luff

MAINSAIL

JIB

headstay

backstay

shrouds

telltale

cunningham hook

tack

window

boom

clew

outhaul

foot

mainsheet
traveler

tack

vang

mainsheet

DECK

STERN

BOW

cockpit

tiller

jibsheet
traveler

HULL

compass (to help
spot wind shifts)

transom

keel

rudder

leech

*The Soling, a class of racing keelboat. This Olympic class boat has more
sail-control lines and hardware than most daysailing dinghies and keelboats.*

CHAPTER ONE

The Wind

Before we attempt the subject of sailing, some things must be said of the wind, since its direction and velocity are of quintessential importance to the sailor. The wind is the one common element of each decision. It dominates every consideration. It animates every alternative. Nothing happens without It. The wind is everything. Sometimes, alone in the night or fog, when references from outside the system are scarce or shut out by intense concentration on the wind, I experience the loss of the rest of my world, and even of myself, to a hypnotic unity with it.

For sailors, the wind's primacy requires that most references to direction refer to the directions whence and whither it blows, such as:

> upwind / downwind
> on the wind / off the wind
> windward / leeward
> weather / lee
> toward / away

The wind is neither ally nor enemy, nor is it neutral. There can be no more perfect indifference than that of nature to us creatures, a cause for wise rejoicing. True achievement

1

lies in the successful adaptation of oneself to reality. We who give ourselves to fashioning such achievement will seek to join our little force with the great one, or to gain our way cunningly against it, or, when neither is possible, to do the only thing left: wait with grace.

Wind is rarely steady in direction or velocity for longer than a few minutes. Local shifts of 10 or 20 degrees, or lulls and gusts on a magnitude of 50 percent below or above the prevailing strength, may occur only moments apart. Winds and calms may appear together in patches. As the wind changes, the efficient sailor responds. Beginners acquire more efficient responses as they gain sensitivity to the wind's variations. Thoroughly learned wind sense is never lost.

The helmsman and crew's weight in this dinghy partially counterbalances the boat's tendency to heel in the wind. The windward shroud telltale, about two feet above the crew's head, reveals that the wind is blowing in over the helmsman's left shoulder, and the boat is sailing nearly as close into the wind as she can manage (Chapter 3). The helmsman holds the mainsheet in one hand, ready to let it run out in a gust of wind (Chapter 9).

The most natural way to sense the wind is by touch. As the wind passes over the exposed parts of one's body—hands, arms, neck, face—small hairs are disturbed, and slight differences in pressure and temperature can be felt. There are also visual clues. Plumes of smoke, flags, and leaves on trees will suggest the wind's general direction. Observation of other sails, or birds (which alight, rest, or take flight facing a wind of any strength), can be helpful. The smallest ripples lie at right angles to the newest wind. Telltale bits of yarn, old nylons, or audio tape may be hung in the rigging, and a wind vane may be mounted at the masthead. Although I have imagined such decorations to slow development of a thorough wind sense, some fine and happy sailors

Telltales sewn or taped onto the luff, or leading edge, of the jib are useful for trimming the jib and when steering to windward, and invaluable when racing. When the sail is trimmed correctly for the course, the windward- and leeward-side telltales stream back horizontally and in parallel. A window in the sail gives a good view of both telltales to the helmsman.

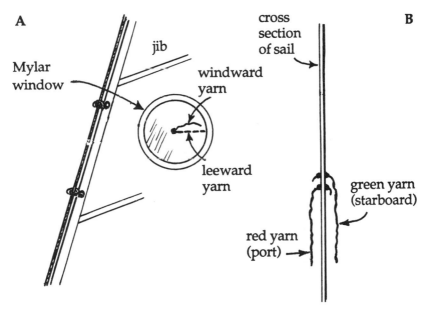

seem to rely on them almost exclusively. Certainly such a wind direction indicator is essential for racing.

Binaural hearing is another valuable sensor, for the sound of the passing wind in one's ears changes as the head is turned. Very likely there exist other indicators beneath the user's conscious threshold. Eventually they combine to create a constant flow of information about the wind, and thereafter one knows without attending to the matter.

In the beginning, you may favor sailing in gentle but persistent breezes, since the lightest winds are both the most variable in direction ("fluky," they are often called) and the most difficult to sense. When other efforts to determine the direction of a moderate breeze have failed, one may simply head into the wind by pushing the tiller toward the side of the boat to which the sails are set, and let the mainsail swing freely inboard. When it settles itself all luffing over the center of the cockpit, the boat's bow is pointing directly into the wind. This is a technique used by racing sailors to test whether a starting line is square to the wind.

The helmsman sitting well to windward has a good view of the jib luff and a good sense of momentary variations in the strength and direction of the wind. The boat is an International One Design, a truly beautiful class of small keelboats.

CHAPTER TWO

Why She Goes

When natural forces combine in subtle ways to produce the unexpected, the result is wonder. The phenomenon of sail is the product of one of those combinations, and even now, after 35 years of sailing, my amazement returns when the quiet power of the system demonstrates itself anew.

The seeming effortlessness of the motive force, underlined by the unaccustomed absence of machinery noises and vibration, is contradicted by the result. Vessel and crew, weighing hundreds or thousands of pounds, are thrust forward continuously, pushing aside tons of water as they rush along together hour after hour, sometimes throwing a bow wave higher than the deck. The archaic metaphors of "plowing" or "furrowing" the sea are as apt as they are poetic. Tilling and sailing both require power, discreetly harnessed and directed.

The system is powered by the air set in motion by the sun's heat, which is what an economist will call a "free good"; anyone may enjoy the benefits of its unlimited use without incurring any production or distribution charge. If you suspect there may be a catch to this arrangement, you are right on two counts.

The first may be chiefly responsible for the egalitarian aspect of the sailing fellowship. The wind belongs equally to the poorest and to the wealthiest of sailors, for when one has none, none may be procured at any price even if its presence in the middle distance can be plainly seen. Moreover, when one has too much, the surplus can neither be sold nor given away, nor even paid to depart, regardless of one's eagerness or status, material or social. All must make do as best they can with whatever wind they get.

The second catch is that in order to use the wind for sailing, the fruits of technology must be acquired. The usual way to do that is by application, liberal or otherwise, of money. Sailmakers and boatbuilders must feed and house families and derive some emoluments from their vocations, or switch to upholstering, plumbing, security sales, or something else all of the rest of us are already doing. Thus would we all be poorer from the added competition and stranded, besides. The impecunious are forced to start small and stay small, a striking though rare example of their scriptural blessedness for, if they will only avoid distracting their attentions from the pleasures at hand by lusting after largeness, they will find that there is more and better sailing to be had from the dinghy than from the vessel that carries it.

Large or small, what is basic to operation of one vessel is equally so to all. The principal technologies are deceptively simple, having been brought to their present state through centuries of incremental efforts by artisans searching for solutions to simple, changeless problems. There are three elements to moving a vessel under sail.

The Wind Pushes on the Sail . . .

The sailmaker constructs a surface shaped in such a way that the force of the wind, striking the impervious surface and changing direction to flow across it, is split into a forward force, called *thrust,* and a sideward force, *drag.* The curve formed by the sail is viewed from above in the accompanying drawing.

The drag is, unfortunately, very large relative to the thrust, which means that sail technology processes wind power into a small, advantageous thrusting force in the

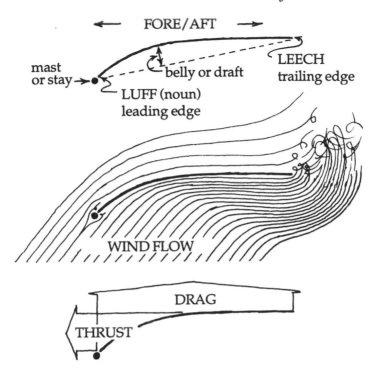

proper direction, and a large, disadvantageous dragging force in the wrong direction entirely. Another technology must be summoned to exorcise the drag, or the helpless sailor will be dragged off to wherever it points.

The Hull Leans Against the Sea ...

The hull designer, after being certain to enclose enough air to float the vessel adequately, and before arranging sundry amenities here and there to attract the appreciation of his market, must cancel nearly all of that large drag force while capitalizing on whatever thrust can be provided by the curve of the sail. This is done by careful shaping of the submerged part of the hull so that it will be pushed most easily by the thrusting force but will greatly resist being pushed by the drag force. Observe the underwater part of any good sailing vessel from ahead. It is fair and sharp, with very little surface presented to either eye or water.

Conversely, a view of the underwater part from abeam presents a very substantial surface, indeed. The area resisting thrust is only a small fraction of that resisting drag.

The sails' drag may heel a boat over plenty as she leans her large underwater profile against the sea, but it won't push her very fast sideways. In fact, heeling in a breeze manifests both a vessel's healthy reluctance to being pushed sideways through the water, and the water's natural resistance to being pushed out of the way by such a large object.

Shoved against the sea by the wind, and made slippery in one direction only, a vessel responds to the presence of even a small forward force by shooting in that direction like a wet watermelon seed squeezed between two fingers.

... and the Crew Puts It Together

The wind-splitting sail is controlled by means of a line called the *sheet*. The sea-pressing hull is controlled by means of the *helm*. By manipulating sheet and helm, the crew dis-

The drawing immediately below shows a hull in sectional view. The same hull viewed in profile—that is, from the side—shows how much greater is resistance to motion sideways than motion forward.

looking forward
from the stern →

looking aft
← from the bow

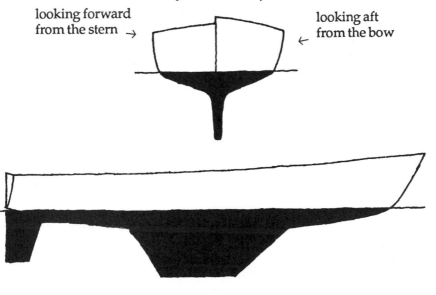

creetly and continuously squeezes the slippery hull between the wind and the sea, with a wondrous and happy result.

In a wheel-steered boat, the helmsman turns the wheel in the direction toward which the boat is to swing. In a tiller-steered boat, the tiller is shoved away from the desired direction of turning. Eric Naranjo shows how it's done on the 41-foot Wind Shadow. *A compass binnacle is mounted just forward of the wheel, and in the foreground the mainsheet, comprising several parts in this fairly large cruising sailboat, is visible.*

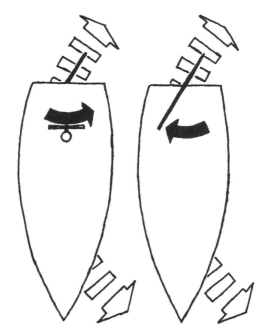

CHAPTER THREE

Sailing

When a sailing craft is moved by thrust created by wind blowing *across* the sail, the driving force is aerodynamic, and that vessel is *sailing*. When no aerodynamic force is present in the sail (as when a vessel is moving in the same direction as the wind and is merely being pushed along), the vessel's movement should not technically be called sailing. A sailor who has given much thought to the process will seldom use the word in its more general, nontechnical sense.

Sailing technique is binary. One of two distinctly different operative modes is employed depending upon which of two distinctly different problems is to be solved in sailing from one place to another.

Reaching

When one desires to direct a vessel's course to any destination lying between approximately 45 and 135 degrees from the wind's origin, one discovers that the course is an easy one. The *tiller* is simply held in the position that points the hull toward the chosen destination.

The helmsman concentrates exclusively on keeping the boat on her proper course, avoiding collision with other vessels, navigation aids, or trap floats, as well as grounding or

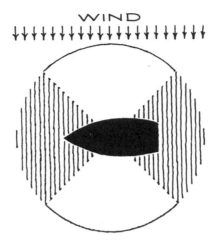

The reaching sector is the shaded portion of the circle.

other embarrassing incidents. Meanwhile, another member of the crew concentrates exclusively on trimming sails to their best performing angle with the wind in order to maximize thrust, so that the boat will move as efficiently as wind and sea allow.

The sail trimmer has the more demanding task. Initially, the sheet must be eased until the sail swings out far enough that its forward part, or *luff* (noun), next to the mast or stay to which it is attached, begins to flutter. In this fluttering condition, the sail is said to *luff* (verb) or to be luffing.

Then the sail is pulled in only until luffing ceases and the sail's curve is full, and *no farther*. The sail is properly trimmed, for the moment.

The attentive sail trimmer will thereafter be occupied with constant observation and testing of the sail to see that it is functioning efficiently. We have noted the inconsistencies of the wind's direction and velocity. Any variation in either of these components causes instant sail inefficiency. If a wind change causes a sail to luff, thrust disappears and the sail must be sheeted in again, as before, to establish its efficient curvature. *But no farther.* Contrarily, if the wind shifts the

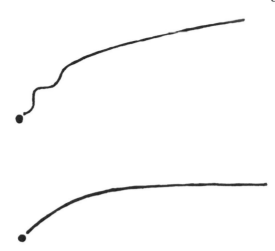

When a boat is reaching, the sail trimmer eases each sail by turn (starting with the forwardmost) until it just begins to luff (top). He then pulls it back in only enough to make the luffing stop (bottom).

other way, that shift will not register at all on a beginner's wind sense. The sail's curve will not change perceptibly when the sail is trimmed too closely for the new wind, but thrust will be greatly reduced, and drag will be increased even more. This is why the sail trimmer conducts regular tests with the sail by easing the sheet (that is, by paying it out in small increments) until luffing barely begins, and then trimming it back to the point of sail efficiency. *But no farther.*

When a vessel carries more than one sail, the foremost is trimmed or eased first, for each sail's trim affects the trim of the following sail.

While the sail trimmer, eyes on the sail, has been growing a stiff neck and regularly fiddling with the sheet to trim or test, the helmsman seems to have been singularly at ease. This is deceptive, because a good helmsman on a reach must, as nearly as possible, sail a straight line. Nothing so thoroughly frustrates one responsible for trimming sails as a helmsman who allows the boat to wander from her course. The effect on the sail of each wandering is exactly the same as that caused by a wind shift, and no sooner has the trimmer corrected for the slovenly course, when it happens again, as the helmsman corrects his error. The wretched crewman, watching only the symptoms with no idea of the cause, is being exercised needlessly by indifferent steering. The wake of a reaching vessel should be straight.

Beating

Sailing's other operative mode is employed when the boat's destination lies to weather, within the angles bearing about 45 degrees from the wind's source. In this case a sailing craft can only arrive by indirection, first sailing as close to the wind as possible in one direction, and then turning directly up into the wind and beyond, holding at the corresponding angle on the *other* side of the wind with the sails now on the other side of the boat's centerline. The destination is never directly ahead until the last leg is being sailed.

The process is called beating. The act of turning the boat at the end of each beating leg is called *tacking*, or *putting about*. In order to beat, the roles of the crew are reversed from those

The beating sector.

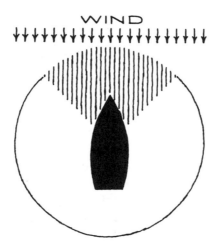

required when reaching. First, the sail is sheeted in as far as easily possible, fastened in that position, and left there. Then, the helmsman, eyes fixed upon the part of the foremost sail which lies along its luff, ignores the boat's course through the water entirely. Instead of watching where the boat is going, either presently or eventually, the helmsman becomes the sail trimmer—but not with the sheet, for that, and the sails, are fixed. Rather, the sails are trimmed and tested by moving the helm, which changes not just the angle between the wind and the sail, but the angle between the wind and the entire vessel.

The wind, as always, is changing. When it changes in one direction, the sail luffs. The helmsman then changes the vessel's heading by *bearing away* from the wind just enough to cause the luffing to stop. *But no farther.* When the wind changes in the other direction, the beating helmsman has no way of knowing without testing for it, which is done at inter-

The process of beating. Each right angle turn represents an instance of tacking, or coming about.

vals by *bearing up* into the wind by very small degrees until the area of the sail near its (noun) luff begins to (verb) luff, and thereupon bearing away just enough to make the whole sail draw again. *But no farther.* The track of a vessel going to weather in the hands of a good helmsman is never a straight line. Its direction curves a bit with each wind change, and also when the vessel is steered very slightly into and out of the wind during the testing process.

Though the former sail trimmer is able now to ignore sail efficiency, beating creates a new duty—that of lookout to see that the boat's course is safe in relation to the rest of the world. The lookout advises the preoccupied helmsman of timely action needed to avoid trouble and, selecting an efficient course to the destination, decides when the next tack should be made. All external considerations are that person's sole responsibility, which allows the helmsman to concentrate on efficiently gaining ground against the wind by minding the entire system, and acquiring a stiff neck of his own.

To summarize the rudiments of sailing: In reaching more or less across the wind, with an infinite number of possible courses, the hull and rudder are, conceptually, a unit pointed at the chosen destination, and the movable sail is constantly adjusted to reconcile the wind's changing velocity and direction with the course (which is, ideally, a straight line). By contrast, in beating upwind, with only two possible wind headings, the hull and the sails are, conceptually, a unit, and the movable rudder is constantly adjusted to keep the sails, the vessel, and the track at their smallest efficient angle relative to the changing wind, regardless of the eventual destination. The track is, therefore, ever-curving.

Thinking in terms of two crew roles is an effective way to identify what has to be attended to on a sailboat, and to make efficient use of the abilities on board. In a singlehanded vessel, naturally, both duties befall the single crew, and neither role may be properly slighted in favor of the other. The beginning sailor will find this situation to be taxing at first, especially on a reach, but practice eases the dual role until it becomes automatic. I have found that the student learns how to sail better (and more quickly) when the roles are separated in the beginning stages. A couple, exchanging responsibilities, learns most quickly.

It is important to note here that a beginning sailor in a small, open centerboarder should never actually fasten the mainsail sheet when beating, unless the breeze is light and steady. The mainsheet should be hand-held, ready to be let out slightly if the boat suddenly heels to an unmanageable or anxiety-producing degree, or to be let go altogether if a strong gust threatens to capsize the boat.

Bear in mind that during a beat or close reach in medium or heavy airs the angle of heel can be precisely controlled by mainsheet adjustment. Easing the main a few inches will put the boat back on her bottom, where she probably sails best, anyway. Often this means carrying a slight mainsail luff in strong winds or in gusts. This is acceptable practice. When one simply can't use all the wind there is, attempting to do so is uncomfortable, if not foolish.

Tacking

One problem that besets some beginning sailors deserves discussion: the problem of tacking poorly. The stronger the wind or the steeper the seas, the more difficulty there is to this operation. Extreme conditions can make tacking light vessels impossible even for master mariners.

Beginners may have trouble tacking with consistent success under *any* conditions. For a few, the problem becomes obsessive, eroding pleasure to the point of disgust. Upon deciding to tack, they alter course attempting to swing the bow through the wind, and for no discernible reason end up pointing directly into the wind, with everything luffing and no steerageway. The rudder seems ineffective. They drift helplessly backward, pumping their tillers from side to side, trying to make their stubborn boats turn. This is called "getting into irons." And just when the perverse critter seems to have gotten out, she sails right back in again.

This situation is entirely avoidable in normal weather and sea states. While tacking, a vessel is momentarily without power. The wind's drag on the hull, rigging, and luffing sails exerts a stopping force, as do waves, which usually come from the same direction as the wind. For the rudder to have any effect, water must be flowing past its surfaces. When the

Tacking a tiller-steered boat. When all are ready, the helmsman puts the tiller to leeward, which pivots the rudder to windward and turns the boat's bow into the wind. The wind is thereby spilled from the sails, which settle, luffing, over the center of the boat. As the turn continues, the sails gradually fill with wind again on the opposite side of the boat, and with the "tack" completed, the boat sails off on her new "tack." This boat started on starboard tack (wind coming in over her starboard side) and wound up on port.

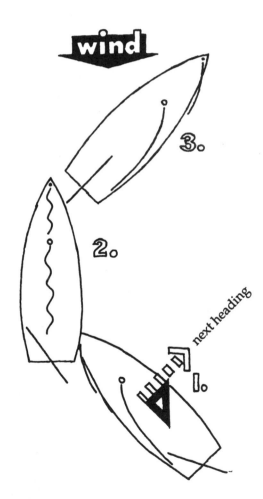

boat has been stopped halfway through a tack, she is *in irons*. For successful tacking every time:

- Start the tack from a beat, not from a reach, in order to minimize luffing time.
- Have enough momentum at the start of the tack to carry the boat through the powerless period. Light vessels require more speed than heavy ones.
- Execute tacks smartly—not necessarily fast, but not slow, either. Slow-motion tacks often fail.
- Know clearly, in advance, the next heading to be sailed. The vessel's bow must turn through a full 90 degrees of central angle, or a bit more. Many helmsmen have a tendency not to turn far enough.

After making sure that the boat is, indeed, on her best close-hauled heading with the sails properly trimmed, one should deliberately choose the proper next heading before beginning the tack. The new heading will lie exactly toward the weather beam. By selecting some reference point there and aiming the bow at it, you will be approximately on the new heading. Better still, select some point directly abeam to leeward and point the stern at it. This is often more convenient because the weather beam is usually behind one's back, and it is good practice, in small, tiller-steered boats, to face aft while crossing to the next steering station on the weather side. As you sail, you will find other tricks for helping your boat tack in difficult circumstances.

Moreover, getting out of irons is easy. It can be done with no help from the sails. The vessel in "stays" (another term for the same condition) is slowly backing down on her rudder. If the rudder is pointed to one side and left there, the stern will slowly swing that way. If the sails have been given plenty of extra sheet, they won't begin to drive until the bow has turned well away from the wind. Then one can trim in the sails. It is important to reverse—or at least center—the rudder the instant the boat begins moving forward, or else she will sail right back into irons, and the entire scene will have

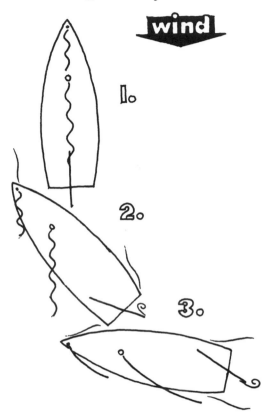

*To get out of irons (1),
let the boat fall back-
ward with sails luffing
freely and tiller pushed
to the side toward
which you wish to
turn (2). When the
sails fill and forward
motion is regained,
bring the tiller back to
windward.*

to be reshot. Holding the boom out or pulling the jib over to the same side the rudder is on will speed the backing and turning process, but it is not necessary. Small, jibless cata-marans are notoriously reluctant to tack, being so light and having so much windage. In a fresh breeze, going into and out of stays is standard procedure for getting them about.

For singlehanding beginners with jibs, there seems too much to do all at once. At the same time the vessel is steered onto a new course, the old lee jibsheet must be released and the new lee jibsheet must be set up. Both hands are required to haul in all the extra sheet, so it seems that the tiller must be held in one's teeth. Not so! With good timing, the helm will take care of itself while the vessel is tacking.

Every boat has her own turning period, which varies a bit with conditions, but there is time enough to do everything, once one has worked out a system. After putting the helm down, the singlehander may abandon it, free the old sheet as the turn begins, and set up the new one as the boat reaches her new course. Meanwhile, the tiller has been slowly returning toward center, so as the singlehander assumes a steering position on the new weather side, the vessel has approximately reached her new course and the nearly centered tiller is ready for grasping before it swings too far the other way. The speed of the tack is varied by how hard the helm is pushed to leeward. Every boat requires a lot of knowing.

CHAPTER FOUR

Running Downwind

When moved by wind simply pushing directly against the sail, and not by the aerodynamic forces created by wind passing across a sail, a boat is not sailing, but *running* before the wind. This condition occurs when a course must be steered to a destination lying more than approximately 135 degrees away from the wind's source.

When running, the driving force is of a markedly different nature. The boat is being moved entirely by the wind's drag on all surfaces—but mostly on the sail, which is spread out as far as seems reasonable in order to maximize drag by presenting as much area as possible to the wind.

With few exceptions, running is less exciting than sailing. The faster the vessel runs, the less wind is felt by both crew and rigging. One knot of added speed downwind reduces the apparent or "felt" wind by exactly that amount. In light to moderate winds, running speed is limited to a lower percentage of the wind's velocity than when sailing.

Running under mainsail and jib requires artful steering and course planning in order to keep both sails working as much as possible. Steering directly downwind allows the mainsail to be boomed out to one side while the wind holds the jib out on the other—"wing-and-wing." Turn a bit to one side and the jib flops over to hang limply in the mainsail's wind shadow. Turn a bit to the other, and the vessel is

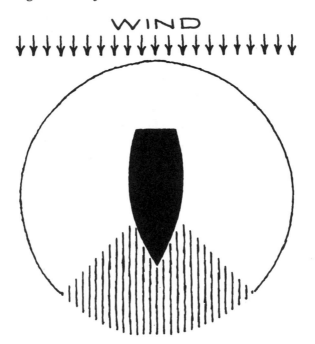

The running sector.

A boat is not really sailing when she is running; she is merely being pushed forward by the wind's drag.

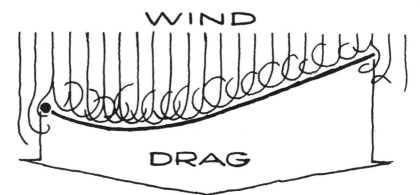

"running-by-the-lee," which means that both the wind and the mainsail are on the same side of the boat. That situation may be the precursor of an unwanted event: Without much warning, the mainsail and its boom could crash over to the lee side. This is called a *jibe*, and, if unexpected, it can be dangerous in a strong wind.

Jibing

A jibe happens when the following wind is brought from one side of the boat to the other. Although tacking also results in changing wind direction from one side to the other, the processes contrast greatly. Tacking brings the wind across the bow, as the boat shifts from beating with the sail sheeted close aboard on one side, to beating with the sail sheeted similarly on the other. The fastened sheet holds the sail inboard at a small angle with the wind. As the turn progresses,

On a downwind leg in intercollegiate competition, these dinghy sailors run wing-and-wing. Sailors on the old working schooners called it "reading both pages." The crewmember in the foreground boat has his hand on the main boom to help guard against an unwanted jibe. The mainsail has been swung outboard as far as it can go, so that the boom has fetched up against the shroud and the mainsheet is slack. On a larger boat, one wouldn't want to let the shrouds take this sort of sideways thrust.

the sail luffs progressively until the boat has made half her turn and is head to wind. The boom is centered. The entire sail luffs. As the turn is completed, the sail fills progressively until the new heading is attained. The event is rather gentle. If the sail is controlled by a single sheet, the sheet is not touched. The carefree quality of tacking arises from the fact that the wind crosses the sail at the luff, which is fastened along its entire length to a spar or stay, and the sail is thus pacified.

Jibing is caused when the wind is allowed to cross the boat's stern—a shift from running with the sail sheeted far out on one side to running with the sail sheeted far out on the other. Luffing does not occur. The wind, having gotten around far enough to the side the sail is on, catches the sail's free, trailing edge—its *leech*—and instantly fills it from behind, causing sail and boom to swing suddenly across the hull and out to the opposite side. Their journey can be violent in a fresh breeze. The stronger the wind, the more carefully mainsail jibes must be planned and controlled, and the more dangerous an unanticipated one becomes—to the boat, as steering is momentarily lost or a shroud parts; and to the crew, who may not realize that it is time to duck and hang on.

Jibing. Having pushed the tiller to starboard to turn the boat downwind (to port) the helmsman releases the port-side jibsheet while the crew quickly takes in the mainsheet. Once the main boom is nearly centered, the helmsman will continue the turn while trimming the starboard-side jibsheet, and the crew will ease the mainsail out to starboard.

You can note the likelihood of a jibe and predict its occurrence by watching the sails. The jib always jibes first. If it was hanging limply ahead of the main, it jibes into a wing-and-wing position. Jibes of unboomed sails are never serious, unless there are crewmembers in the way. As the wind gets a bit farther around to the side the boom is on, the mainsail's leech becomes restless and its *clew* (its after, lower corner) tends to rise. The moment has come either to head up a bit to prevent the jibe from occurring, or to jibe the sail properly.

In a small boat, the best technique for jibing is to put the wind dead astern and haul in the mainsail—not by trimming the sheet in, but by grabbing together all the sheet's parts at once and hauling it in overhand, simultaneously pulling downward to keep the boom from lifting. As the mainsail passes the midpoint and begins to fill, it should be let go completely to swing as it will to the full length of its free sheet, without any hindrance.

When jibed carelessly in a fresh breeze, small, unballasted boats tend to capsize, which is a separate adventure.

In jibing larger craft, technique is not quite so critical. The helmsman concentrates on holding the difficult course directly downwind while the crew hauls in the sheet in the conventional manner, letting it run freely to the other side the moment it will. This requires the sheet to be clear to run—no kinks or knots, and no turns around anyone's ankles. In either procedure, the boom should arrive amidships under downward tension and without momentum, and be completely free to swing out.

Other Considerations

You may have concluded from the foregoing that, in trying to run efficiently with all sails drawing, the number of possible courses is nearly as limited as it was in beating. This is true. There are other similarities as well. Once again, the helmsman must watch the jib. If it is sometimes slightly restless, all is well, but the jib must not get too restless, for then it will jibe behind the main and cease working. It is when the jib pulls quietly that the main must be watched for the telltale signs of a jibe. All the while, as in beating, the sheets are fastened, and the helmsman, with full attention on the sails, adjusts their trim with the helm. The course is seldom straight for very long.

If the run is expected to be long enough, much of the steering constraint necessary to avoid jibing can be eliminated by use of a preventer on the main boom and a whisker pole between jib clew and boat to hold the jib in a winged-out position. A whisker pole can be jury rigged from a boathook, spinnaker pole, or paddle if need be. Preventers will be discussed further in Chapter 8.

When wind and seas are high, running under jib alone is a blessing. It is both possible and, at times, propitious, to run with no sail at all, employing only the wind's drag on the hull and rigging. The boat's speed is thereby greatly reduced, yet a surprising amount of directional control can be retained.

Running is characterized by reduced stability. When sailing, drag resistance by the hull causes heeling, but as the

The process of tacking downwind. Each turn represents a jibe. In a very light breeze a boat might find it advantageous to jibe through 90 degrees as shown, but a shallower jibing angle is usually sufficient in moderate wind.

heeling angle increases, the hull's inherent resistance to further heeling also grows. For each point of sail and wind velocity, an angle of heel is established at which the boat is pressed over as far as she will be, and held there. Rolling motion disappears, and a feeling of stiffness takes its place. This is the incentive for the small "steadying sail" set by many commercial fishing vessels at sea. That good effect is absent when running. Even small seas cause a running vessel to roll from side to side, sometimes uncomfortably.

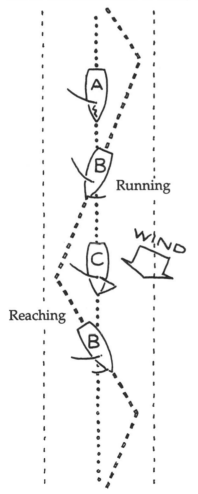

Running in a channel when the wind won't quite let the jib draw but won't quite let you sail either (boat A) is boring! Running and reaching (boat B) keeps both sails full. Note that the mainsail stays on the same side. Only the jib is jibed. Running in a channel using a whisker pole to hold out the jib (boat C) is often possible when the jib will not quite set wing-and-wing of its own accord. Boat B will quickly leave A behind, and will probably outdistance C if of similar size.

When a boat is running in rough water, waves striking the stern and rudder at various angles from behind tend to knock her off her proper course. This condition combines with the rolling motion to create course-holding difficulty, which demands attentive steering, especially with wind directly astern. For this reason, among others, many sailors prefer not to run directly before the wind but to gain stability and reduce anxiety by *sailing* downwind in a series of very broad reaches, called "tacking downwind." In this process, the boat is jibed at the end of each leg to bring the wind on the other side, and, as with beating, only on the final leg is the destination over the bow. Running and reaching are frequently combined to solve certain course-keeping problems.

One more note on the relationship between tacking and jibing: The casual sailor intent on circling a mark soon discovers that the choice of which way to go around involves a choice between tacking or jibing.

Rounding a buoy or other mark will necessitate a tack or a jibe depending on the direction of the turn.

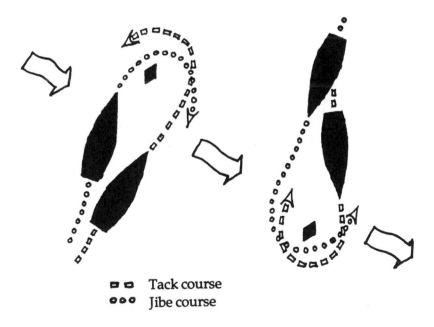

🔲 🔲   Tack course
●●●   Jibe course

CHAPTER FIVE

The Apparent Wind and Sail Trim

One difference between novices and experienced sailors is that the former are frequently mystified by unexpected behavior of the sail or the boat, while the latter's mystification is only occasional. The cause can usually be traced to an effect of the wind, the current, or, rarely, some other external force. The wind is the most likely culprit because of its propensity for frequent change, often without easily recognized warning.

The true wind is never sensed by an object in motion; even a pedestrian must stand still to feel true wind. The apparent or felt wind is the true wind as altered by the motion of the vessel through it.

To clarify the effect of motion on apparent wind, assume the boat to be stationary in the water with the wind nearly abeam, the boom swung out to the other side as far as possible, and all sails luffing entirely. The wind now felt is the true wind. Then the sail is trimmed properly, which causes forward motion. As the boat gathers way, the sail begins to luff because, with movement, the wind no longer appears to be coming from abeam but from a little ahead of the beam, even though neither the helmsman nor the wind has changed heading. So the sail is again trimmed to this "new" wind, and the boat responds with further acceleration, which causes the felt wind to apparently draw still farther ahead, creating another luff and requiring more trimming, until the force of the sail's thrust is equalled by the water's resistance to further acceleration. At that point, the boat is doing as well as possible on that particular heading, in that state of sea, with that particular wind velocity and sail combination. Though the true wind is still nearly abeam, the apparent wind is ahead of the beam by an angular distance proportionate to boat speed.

Proper sail trim thus depends not only upon a boat's heading in relation to the direction of the true wind, but varies also with speed through the true wind. Proper sail trim relates entirely to *apparent* wind. When two well-trimmed sailboats are sailing on a common course through a common wind, the sails of the one moving faster will be trimmed more closely than those of the slower. Planing hulls, such as catamarans, with their greatly reduced water resistance, may, in a 20-knot breeze, reach a speed equal to that of the wind, with the sail sheeted close aboard, as though beating, almost regardless of the true wind heading. The most extreme example is an iceboat, which, with no significant resistance to forward motion, may attain speeds of 50 or more knots in a fresh breeze, going nearly downwind close-hauled, with apparent wind nearly ahead.

On the other hand, consider a boat beating along with fair speed despite a rather light and uncertain wind. Suddenly she enters an area of calm (a common phenomenon). The effect on the sail is one of sudden, complete luffing, as the momentum of the boat converts the still air into an apparent wind ahead. The effect on the novice is to cause a reflexive "bearing off" in a vain search to fill the sail with wind that isn't there. The sail refuses to fill. No matter which way the craft is steered, the "wind" seems to perversely anticipate each turn by staying directly ahead, until, as momentum disappears, all way is lost, giving the sailor literal pause to contemplate the lesson. Whenever a light wind seems to draw ahead suddenly, a calm or *lull* may be suspected.

A change in one aspect of the wind—velocity or direction—is often accompanied by a change in the other; hence, a diagnosis of what happened can be complex. If one adds to wind changes a strong current or eddy and, perhaps, inexpert steering, diagnosis may be impossible. Luffing is caused by one—or any combination—of the following: steering too high; trimming too broadly; the wind's shifting more ahead; a decrease in wind velocity (a lull); or a current, eddy, or wave pitching the boat ahead.

Conversely, a sudden increase in wind velocity (a gust) often causes unexpected heeling. The boat is not moving rapidly enough for the new wind, and the sail is trimmed too closely to use the gust for thrust. The vessel responds by heeling with the sudden load of new drag. Proper crew response is either to steer higher or to start the sheet. Both acts spill excess wind and allow the helm to regain steering control, which is often lost when heeling beyond reason. Whenever the sail is trimmed too closely for the wind and course—a condition amusingly called sailing "bare"—the effect is excessive heel and sideward drift (*leeway*) due to excessive drag, with loss of efficient thrust. In light or moderate airs, heeling response to bare trimming is absent. The only way to sense the condition without the subtle signs that come with experience is to test for it with helm or sheet.

Sailing bare is caused by one—or a combination—of the following: steering too low; over-trimming; the wind's shifting more aft; increased wind velocity; or the boat's being suddenly slowed by current, eddy, or a sea smacking the bow.

CHAPTER SIX

Getting Away From and Back To It All

You are a cooler character than I if you can go sailing for the first time as skipper of an unknown sailboat, especially your own, without a rush of buck fever. The signs are all there—heart pounding, fingers trembling, mouth dry, impatience with small things, heightened, slightly defective reception of stimuli—but they can be overcome by deliberately slowing down and taking one step at a time in proper order. Procedural order is paramount for getting underway gracefully. First, always, one must contemplate the wind.

Getting Underway

The boat should be turned to face the wind while the mainsail is being raised—and the main is, with one exception, the first sail to be set. Then, if desired, the jib may be set. At that point the boat may be freed of her last restraint, the bow line, to fall off the wind until her sails fill and she sails away. This type of start is most conveniently accomplished from a mooring, since it is the nature of boats to *lie to* the wind (that is, to keep the bow facing the wind) when fastened at the bow alone, unless there is an overpowering current. One merely needs to get on sail and, when a swing puts the wind on the desired side, let go the mooring or break out the anchor and bear away.

A berth at a pier or wharf complicates the matter. Except by coincidence, the wind probably is not coming from ahead. Even if it is, some sea room must be arranged; the boat must be handed out, or handed along, until the bow can be snubbed with room astern. This method not only will hold her facing the wind while the sail is raised, but will provide a place from which she can be sailed away much as though it were a mooring.

When the wind blows directly or obliquely onto the face of a wharf, getting away takes a bit more doing, since often the boat cannot be handed along by her crew to a more favorable place. Engine power is then a great convenience for maneuvering out and facing upwind. A small boat may often be paddled off the weather face of a dock or beach in mild conditions and anchored with room to swing as the sails are hoisted. Failing those possibilities, it may be necessary to set an anchor some distance off and haul the boat away from her berth.

Hoisting the mainsail first and with the bow pointing directly into the wind keeps the action aboard relaxed and orderly. If the jib were raised first, the bow would want to swing off the wind, allowing the sails to fill and start drawing. It would then soon be necessary to start fending off the pier and other boats.

A jib, alone, gives good control anywhere downwind. When circumstances preclude turning about to face the wind and there is an appropriate path downwind, one may run out under jib only, because that sail can be raised regardless of wind heading. This is the only occasion on which the jib is the first sail raised. In a cat-rigged boat, the top of the sail, raised a little way up the mast, works in a similar way. When sea room is attained the boat may be anchored or, with some experience, rounded up while the mainsail is set.

A small boat under mainsail alone can be backed dead to leeward for any distance by keeping the sail fully luffing. This is done by pointing the rudder to mimic the positions of the very loose-sheeted boom as it swings first to one side, then the other. This keeps the stern approximately under the end of the boom. If you recognize this process as purposely staying in irons—good for you! One gets out in the normal fashion: When the course is clear, turn the rudder to the side opposite that toward which you want the bow to swing (because the water is now pushing the rudder from behind). Remember that the moment the sail fills with forward drive, the rudder must be reversed. Backing under sail should not be tried without several practice sessions away from obstructions, in various wind velocities. Some boats do better than others. Remember that a wind shift can erase your intended safe course.

In a larger boat with which he is unfamiliar, the sailor should clear all obstructions under engine power before raising any sails. Vessels equipped with single-screw inboard engines are notoriously unreliable at backing under power. They tend to back to port, with bows swinging to starboard, and some ignore their helms entirely. It is seldom possible to make accurate predictions under all conditions without intimate knowledge of the boat. Outboard engines swivel, which allows for easy maneuvering.

Hoisting a mainsail full of wind is an unseamanlike affair if it can be done at all. Pressure in the sail causes slides to stick in the mast track, battens to become entangled with the rigging, and the bellying sail to rub the spreaders and shrouds. To add insult, a sail full of wind makes the boat want to sail, and if she cannot, she tugs at her restraints, heels, and exhibits hyperactive tendencies. The only sensible way to hoist a masted sail is to do it while facing into the wind so that the sail will be hoisted all luffing from start to finish. Then the slides or bolt rope shake loose from friction and the sail is free to hoist. But even then, someone must look aloft to be certain that there will be no surprises.

Raising a sail is a critical moment in the sailing process. When the sails are up, the "engine" is running. When the wind gets into them, the engine is "in gear." Sailboats have no brakes. Before hoisting sails, repeat the following ritual, every time:

Is this sail ready to hoist? Stops, ties, or gaskets are removed, no stray reef points are left tied or untied, sail battens are in place, the outhaul is properly tensioned, and the downhaul and boom vang are freed. (All of these sail-shape

A sailor looks aloft while raising sails.

controls will be discussed in Chapter 8.) Jib snaps are all in proper order with none skipped or backward, the tack is fast to the stem, and jibsheets are securely fastened to the clew.

Are both ends of the halyard secured? The working end, attached to the sail's head, must not come adrift or it may be lost up the mast. The free end, or tail, must be fastened to something on the mast or deck or it may be lost up the mast or to the wind. Either event can provoke merriment among the audience as the skipper lowers the mast, or climbs it, to retrieve the business end, stares stupidly at the whole halyard lying in a heap at his feet, or stumbles about the vessel waving a boathook in the air to coax the windblown streamer down to its duty station.

Is the sheet free, clear, and ready to run properly through its blocks? There should be no knots or kinks in the line. A sail cannot be fully raised against a taut sheet. The boom or foot must be free to rise and swing where it will, to keep the sail fully luffing until power is wanted. Make sure there is plenty

Such everyday embarrassments as getting the halyard wrapped around a spreader or wedging the tip of a batten (see photograph, page 76) behind a shroud result if one fails to look aloft while raising sails.

of slack in the sheets. Some perfectionists make up the off-duty mainsheet into a neat, elaborate hank, to be hung on the boom for aesthetic effect when the vessel is berthed. Ah, vanity! Forgetting to unmake the bauble until the boat is underway can lead to frantic clawing at the knotty mess in the effort to let enough wind out of the sail to stop the vessel from crashing into things. There should be only one knot in every sheet—at the very end, so that it won't be lost overboard.

Is the helm free and ready to steer with? Tillers are often tied and wheels locked, to keep the rudder from working when the boat is idle.

Is the halyard clear to run properly? It must not be turned around any of the rigging aloft, or caught behind a spreader. Jib halyards tend to get wrapped around the headstay—a condition that can easily escape notice.

Only now are you ready to hoist with care. Unexpected resistance must be investigated before proceeding. Look aloft while hauling. Masted sails should be "two-blocked," that is, hauled to their very limit. Low sails and booms are the mark of novices. Rope halyards should be stretched or they will stretch later, allowing the luff to loosen, necessitating retensioning while underway. (Nylon is never used for halyards, because of its elasticity.) The main's halyard is belayed conventionally to starboard, but in any case, hank and hang it in such a way that it will be ready to run instantly when it is time that the sail be lowered. Tension the boom downhaul as necessary. Take your time. Do it properly and thoughtfully; there is no need to hurry.

The jib's *tack* (forecorner) is normally fast to its fitting at the stem, so its luff is tensioned by the halyard. After pulling in the proper degree of tension, or a little more if the halyard is of rope, belay to port, and hank and hang it for running.

The moment to begin sailing is at hand. Choose the best direction. Let go the bow when it swings that way, if on a mooring, or push it that way if a dock or piling is handy to push against. A positive mooring departure is accomplished by walking aft, pulling the mooring line along the side of the vessel, and dropping it once forward motion and steerage-

This jib's luff is equipped with hanks, spring-loaded clips that fasten conveniently around the headstay. The tack is made fast to a stem fitting by a snap shackle. Partially visible is a welded-rod bow pulpit to contain crewmembers, a common feature on cruising sailboats. A lightweight Danforth anchor is stowed on the pulpit, out of the way but ready to use.

way have been created. If you are singlehanded, move carefully and without undue haste to the helm. Nothing much will happen before you get there. The sails won't fill immediately because you gave them plenty of extra sheet. Upon gaining the helm, trim the sheets (do the jib first) and steer away.

Maneuvering

While piloting close to obstructions in a harbor or anchorage, the crew should keenly observe surrounding circumstances and plan each move far in advance, along with alternatives in the event plans must change. Trouble lurks where there is neither sea room nor alternative. Thinking time is gained by slowing without losing steerageway—either by luffing or sailing bare.

Turning boats rotate about a vertical axis somewhere near the middle of the hull. The stern swings about as far in one direction as the bow swings in the other. Turning without enough room will bang the stern against whatever occupies the swinging space. To mar one's own topsides is a peccadillo, but to mar another's is a cardinal sin to be remembered forever with humiliation. I do.

Under ideal conditions, if the turn is made into the wind, a slowly moving sailboat can turn completely about in its own length. One may help the head around in tight places, or force the bow in a desired direction, by "backing the jib," which means to haul it over to the wrong side by sheet or, better still, by hand, so that the wind gets into the front of it, pressing it backward. This causes the bow to swing in the direction opposite to which the jib is held. If the mainsail is given all its sheet, it will not begin to drive the boat until she is nearly around.

Sometimes jibing *seems* the most practical way to turn a sailboat around, but unless there is *plenty* of room for the maneuver—at least twice as much as one would imagine to be needed—this is a mistake. One does not notice how much distance a jibe uses up when distance is immaterial. Dawning recognition of the oversight when well into an irrevocable, disastrously calculated jibe is indescribably painful, even for the inevitable spectators.

Getting Back

Returning to a mooring is somewhat the reverse of leaving it. The normal approach is upwind, for at the moment of arrival forward momentum must be exhausted, with sails all luffing. This requires a good guess of the boat's carrying distance without power in that particular condition of wind, sea, and current. Controlling factors are the approach speed and the length of your boathook. Errors cost only another try, since slowly overrunning a mooring will cause no damage.

When the wind blows from the dock the same approach may be employed—or the dock may be approached obliquely, on a close reach. In the latter case, with the jib struck, the mainsheet may be played in and out to produce, reduce, or cut thrust as needed. It is best, with this method, to grab all its parts together in hand for quick, sure response, just as you might do for jibing. Even when a mainsail seems to be all luffing, some unwanted thrust often remains. Sometimes the boom must be pushed out by hand to get rid of thrust completely. Upwind landings can be aborted and attempted again if doubts arise, and there is sea room.

Downwind landings cannot be aborted. Go directly upwind from the landing spot and strike your sails before turning to run down under bare mast. You will go slowly—though not as slowly as you might wish at the very last moment—and, in the absence of a strong crosscurrent, you will have directional control to reach your target. If you need a little more speed for control, you can temporarily raise or hold up a few feet of sail, but don't overdo it. Speed is what you won't want.

A sailor's best virtue is patience, and a sailor's best friend is a proper anchor—unless there is a reliable engine aboard. The latter can often substitute for both. Under engine power, with reverse gear, any slowly moving boat does have brakes. Maneuvering safely around docks, piers, and other vessels, however, whether under either sail or engine power, requires caution and a certain humility or, failing those, infallibility.

CHAPTER SEVEN

Putting It All Together

Let us imagine a first sail. Though it is hardly possible that your real first sail will resemble this one, the same technical responses are required through a broad range of circumstances. We will, of course, choose a pleasant, gentle day for this sail, with no rough weather forecast.

If there is a nautical chart of the waters in which you plan to learn, procure a copy for study. Note shoals, obstructions, and piloting aids. Compare the chart's markings with what you can see from land. Even if you are sailing in familiar waters, plan your course from start to finish.

Included here is a chart to help us visualize our imaginary adventure. We plan to sail around that little island just beyond the harbor entrance, returning along the shoals to the east. Let's examine the wind. The flag on the marina office indicates that here in the harbor the wind is mild and steady from a little west of north. There are no whitecaps on the bay, and those boats we see seem to be sailing on the same wind, so we conclude that conditions are about the same outside the basin. Our scan of the horizon reveals no impending change. This seems a good time to spread the wings of our imaginary 16-foot centerboard sloop, *Trial And Error*.

To raise sail, we must hand her around to the end of the dock so she can face the wind. Loop the bow line about the corner piling and fasten it back aboard for easy cast-off.

Lower the centerboard. At this point we observe the precautions outlined in the preceding chapter to hoist sail with a minimum of fuss.

Once the sails are raised all the way, and halyards tensioned and secured, remove the bow line and shove off to port. Hauling the sheets just enough to stop luffing (jibsheet first) sends us close reaching toward the other side of the basin.

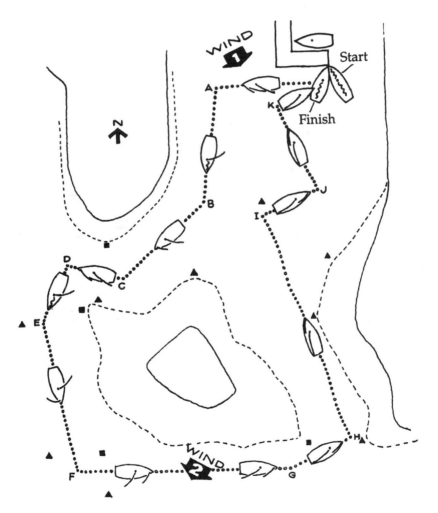

As planned, at point A we fall off the wind to run down for a turning point into the little crooked channel north of the island. The jib, blanketed by the main, won't fill, but this is a short leg and in any event we need time to think about the feel of the wind for a moment while we are so slowed.

Summon your wind sensitivity. Feel the light air movement on the back of your neck, hair, and ears. Hardly there, is it? Note its direction just off the starboard quarter. Remember, the small wind ripples crest at right angles to the wind direction. The flag back at the marina is still visible, too. Turn your head to sense the wind on your cheek. Now we are approaching the turning point (B). If you will continue concentrating on the feel of the wind, you will be able to sense, exactly, the magic moment when, turning but without any sail adjustment, we stop running and start sailing. The jib, of course, will come to life, possibly with a "pop," but that's not what I'm after. I want you to feel the difference in the wind's quality as we slowly—there! Not only does the boat come to life, so does the wind. This is sailing!

Now we trim the sails for the course, and the bubbles speed by the lee rail. Notice we have a little heel, which was not there before. Listen to the murmur of our new bow wave. At point C we trim in the sails some more as we point higher, into a close reach. The response is immediate. The wind is ahead, feeling much stronger as we heel to it. Foam begins to rush by the rail and we can hear the water gurgling along the hull. We wish we could do this all morning, but here is our turning point (D) for going south along the island. We pay out sheets. The wind seems to die. We slow down. The jib quits. To reduce underwater resistance we raise the unneeded centerboard. The sun feels warm. Things get quiet. We'll hold this course until point E, when we can fill the jib to run wing-and-wing and still stay in the channel.

Approaching point F, we partially lower the centerboard for the coming broad reach, and anticipate that the mainsail will jibe during our turn eastward. The telltale on the backstay lets you know when we're by the lee, if you can't feel it yet. As the main's leech begins to flutter restlessly, announcing the jibe, you grab the whole sheet, pulling down to help the boom over, then let go and trim in.

We're sailing again. Good feeling. Nearly a beam reach. Soon the wind lightens. Is it because we're getting into the island's lee? No. We're sailing into a wind shift. There's a gust showing on the surface ahead. The sail beyond the island is heeling to the new wind—and here it is, a veer to the northeast, and a freshening. Our sails luff as the wind moves ahead, so we trim them in. Now we're close reaching, with our weights to weather (that is, to windward) to keep the boat more upright, still heading east. We need more centerboard and might as well lower it all the way to prepare to beat.

Feels like about 15 knots of wind, but let's deduct for overestimation and say 12. The shift should let us fetch the east channel in one long starboard tack. First, we'll sheet in to sail close-hauled (G) so that we can tack easily. Watch the jib and sail as high as you can without slowing down. Now, before we sail onto this shoal ahead, pick your new course on the weather beam. That mark? OK. "Helm alee!" Pushing the tiller to leeward, throwing off the starboard jibsheet, and setting up the port jibsheet, we're on our way northward. While you watch the luff of the jib to keep her moving, I'll see that we safely pass that mark on the edge of the shoal.

Soon we approach point I, ready to begin a port tack into the harbor. The wind lightens noticeably and gets fickle as we get into the lee of the harbor. We drop the jib to slow us still more as we approach point K for the final tack, under main alone. Then we turn up into the wind to coast up to the dock with the mainsheet cast off and the sail dutifully luffing. Congratulations . . . a perfect landing!

Now return to the beginning of our little scenario for a rerun or two. Think about the course in terms of different winds. What if we had sailed around again with the new wind? If the wind had *backed* (shifted in a counterclockwise direction) to the west instead of *veering* to the east, we could have reached up the east channel and luffed right into our berth. What might have been our track had the winds blown from opposite directions? How might we have managed our sail raising and return? This kind of thought process is the sailor's constant occupation.

CHAPTER EIGHT

The Shaping Power

Our culture has chosen sails to be the graphic symbol for boating in general—and for sailing in particular—and for escape from the constraints of life on land. Sails are aesthetically exciting because they are simply and beautifully shaped: smooth, white, hard-edged, steep-sided geometric forms against the sky. Curved to cast clean shadows upon themselves, they express the presence and angle of light, matching the clouds—worthy symbols of romantic aspirations.

The thoughtful sailor, while acknowledging their place in our culture and being rather taken by their attributes, knows regretfully that sails are a poor, inefficient power system, though the only one suiting his purpose. Most of the wind's force is wasted in drag. What little remains is poorly used under the best of conditions. Further disadvantage comes from the many very different conditions through which the entire mechanism must, somehow, function. A vessel designed to function optimally in one combination of circumstances is likely to function poorly under contrasting ones. Therefore, only limited design specialization is practical. The crew must be able to adapt the sail plan, by changing both size and shape, to function as efficiently as its inherent qualities allow in the conditions at hand.

The wind's two essential components, direction and velocity, play the same part in every efficiency equation.

Though effects of a variation in velocity are more extreme and dramatic, changes in the boat's angle to the wind, requiring constant responses from her crew, must be more frequently dealt with.

Most sail material is tightly woven of well-twisted polyester yarn, often heavily sized, resulting in incredibly strong, impermeable cloth of great dimensional stability. The sailmaker constructs the sail by sewing carefully shaped pieces of this cloth together, with each segment oriented to the major lines of force running through its particular part of the sail, in order to minimize potential bias stretch. No matter how fully these two technologies of cloth manufacture and sail fabrication are perfected, however, or how perfectly they are wed, some stretch remains (which is not entirely disadvantageous, as shall be seen).

A sail, when tensioned, stretches along the bias. While a certain amount of this stretching moves the position of the maximum draft forward, giving the sail a more efficient shape for fresher breezes, too much dimensional instability ruins sail shape. New developments in sail materials, such as the use of Mylar and Kevlar, seek to increase dimensional stability.

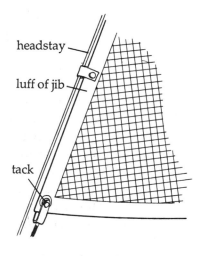
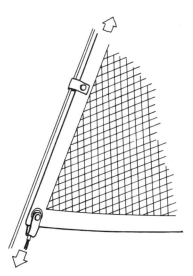

Twist

The chief qualitative defect in cloth sails is their lack of rigidity, which is the basis for a series of difficulties. A sail full of wind tends to "twist" so that the top part is freer than the bottom part. The tendency is least apparent when beating, since the sheet, hauling the sail close aboard, exerts all of its tension in a downward direction. This downward pull, transmitted throughout the sail, results in its shape being rather flat—the *leech* (trailing edge), tightened by the downward pull, lies in nearly the same plane with both *foot* (lower edge) and luff.

When the sheet is payed out even a little bit to accommodate a reach, the downward pull is greatly decreased. That allows the *clew* (lower aft corner) to rise in proportion to both

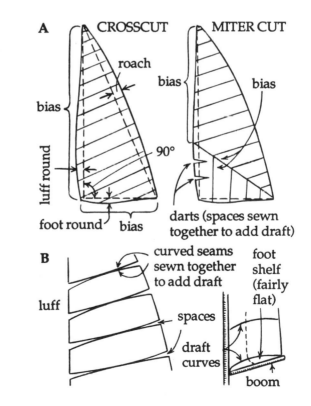

Some common sail cuts.

the broadness of the reach and the velocity of the wind. As
the clew rises, the curve of the leech increases and the top
part of the sail sags forward, creating a twisted sail plane.
When the reach is broad, or when running with a fresh
breeze without any downward pull at all, the end of the
mainsail boom rises quite high as the wind "bellies" the sail,
so that its top may even get ahead of the mast. To keep the
top of the sail from luffing badly, the sheet trimmer must
overtrim the bottom part of the sail. This response is poor,

*Close-hauled, the mainsheet applies considerable downward tension to the
sail, giving it a good, flat shape. Helmsman and crew have their feet under
a hiking strap, the better to lean out to windward and balance the boat.
They are not entirely successful, however, because the boat is heeling and
carrying a weather helm (a tendency to round up into the wind, as explained in Chapter Nine), which the helmsman must counteract by offset-
ting the rudder to leeward.*

however, for three reasons: both sail balance and lateral (heeling) trim are destroyed; excessive leeway is caused; and excessive heeling creates such fierce weather helm that the boat slows (which accents the overtrimming) and steering control often is temporarily lost (which means, among other things, that the desired straight course cannot be steered).

One cannot minimize the effects of sail twist. One must get rid of it. This is accomplished in different ways for boomed and unboomed sails.

Mainsail Twist

A mainsail causing the horrors listed above—and the mainsail is the chief culprit in any heeling problem—must be flattened by a device known as a *boom vang*. This is a small tackle fastened at one end to the lower side of the boom somewhere ahead of its middle, and at the other end to a place near the foot of the mast, if permanent, or to some

Off the wind, the downward tension exerted on the sail by the mainsheet is slight, and the boom may thus rise, allowing the top of the sail to twist forward and start to luff unless overtrimmed. This tendency can be counteracted with a boom vang.

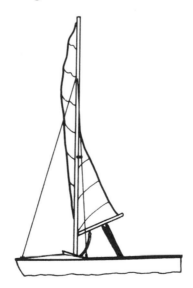

position forward along the lee rail, if occasional. Sufficiently tensioned, this tackle exerts the downward pressure on the boom needed to flatten the sail when neither mainsheet nor gravity can manage the task. Flattening the sail allows the upper and lower parts to be trimmed alike; that way the top neither sags nor luffs, the center doesn't belly, and the bottom doesn't generate miseries. The entire sail works for the vessel the way it should.

Some uninformed, casual sailors decry the boom vang as a nuisance, an added complication. "That's a 'go-fast,' " they say, "strictly for racing!" The boat does move better with one, and competition without is hopeless, but the vang is as much for comfort as for speed. When led to a position on the rail abeam of the mast, it serves as the mainsail jibe preventer while running. In my view, any sailboat's rigging is incomplete without one.

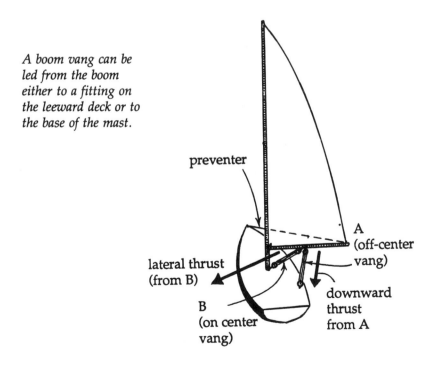

A boom vang can be led from the boom either to a fitting on the leeward deck or to the base of the mast.

preventer

lateral thrust
(from B)

B
(on center
vang)

A
(off-center
vang)

downward
thrust
from A

Headsail Twist

Twist in unboomed headsails may be eliminated simply by trimming to a sheet lead (a block, or sometimes simply an eye) positioned so that the sail has no twist. This requires that the sheet's lead point be changed according to the angle and force of the apparent wind, a simple task that is accomplished by selecting a new lead or, if the lead in use is mounted on a track, by changing its position. Thus, with each major alteration of wind or boat heading, the jib trimmer must adjust the jib's lead as well as its sheet. The criterion for perfect trim will clarify the issue. When a properly trimmed jib is caused to luff slightly, it luffs symmetrically along its leading edge. It may luff simultaneously along its entire length, which is ideal, or it may luff at each end, or luffing may begin in its center and progress evenly toward

A slide-mounted jibsheet lead can be moved forward or aft to compensate for course changes. Racing sailors also make adjustments for the wind velocity when beating, the objective once again being to achieve an efficiently shaped sail that luffs symmetrically along its leading edge. This skipper has taken it a step further with a lead that will slide not only forward and aft, but also toward and away from the boat's centerline, a configuration normally resorted to only by serious one-design racing sailors.

both ends. For symmetrical luffing to occur, tension along the leech and foot must be equal. If the foot is too tight, the top will luff first (the same kind of twist found in mainsails). If the leech is too tight, the bottom will luff first (a kind of reverse twist).

Direct observation of the jib while a course is altered with respect to the wind is the simplest way to learn. Let's assume we are out on our boat again, and that we are beating.

In order to tension the leech and foot equally, the lead must be rather far aft on its track. Mark the spot, for this sail will always require that lead position on a beat in such wind. The foot displays that lovely curve by which the sail's drive is created, and the leech shows about the same curve as well. Both curves are rather flat, which is characteristic of a beat. If the wind were to lighten appreciably, the curves would be increased by easing the sheet and, since the foot is shorter than the leech, by moving the lead slightly forward.

As we head off the wind to reach, we ease the sheet. The clew rises slightly but the foot stays quite flat because of the aftward pull from the old lead. The leech, however, now has a rather large curve, and a little luff appears near its head. This indicates that the leech is too loose and the foot is too tight. The lead must be moved forward to straighten the leech somewhat by exerting more downward pull, which will also induce a proper curve in the foot due to less aftward tension. Each time we head farther downwind, the same thing happens, requiring more forward repositioning of the lead. Finally, when we are nearly running, the lead has gotten rather far forward, and the curves of the foot and leech, though grown voluptuous, are still even.

Altering Sail Shape

Because variations in wind velocity are responsible for the widest disparities in sailing conditions, the sailor's repertoire for properly dealing with them must be equally varied. There are two major responses: altering sail shape or changing sail size.

Sail shape can be modified considerably by varying tension along the edges of the sail. In light airs, the sails should be "baggy," with deepest possible draft or belly. Boom downhauls should be cast off. Headsail halyards should be slightly eased, relieving luff tension. Clew outhauls should be slacked to relax foot tension, and vangs, also, eased to relieve tension along the leech. As the elasticity of the sail material shortens the distances between corners, the shapes of the sails will become fuller. Also, sheets should be eased slightly. A vessel cannot sail as close-hauled in light winds as it otherwise can. On boats that allow the mainsheet lead block to be moved from side to side on a traveler, it should ordinarily be centered in light air, giving the sail more curve.

Racing sailors, who either learn to appreciate the advantages of sail shape control or lose every race, often carry

Some boats have mainsheet travelers. These allow the lead to be moved to leeward in a fresh breeze, exerting more downward tension and helping to flatten the sail. This skipper will move his lead farther to leeward as the breeze freshens.

alternate mainsails cut for differing conditions. Some racing mainsails sport zipper arrangements along the foot by which sail material can be added or subtracted.

When the wind blows hard, sails should be flattened. The mainsail lead point should be repositioned farther toward the lee rail, and all the adjustments made to relieve tension must be reversed to increase it. But tension should not be over-done. Cotton sails of the past had to be brutalized because of their elasticity; no matter how flat they were made, the wind's weight could stretch in some unwanted draft. Polyester sails have no serious dimension problem and far less elasticity. They stay more or less as they are put. Many overstressings will finally tire the material, destroying the sail shape so carefully created by their makers. For long, efficient sail life, it is better to put in not quite enough tension rather than too much.

Wrinkles or creases at right angles to the luff or foot indicate too little tension, as do scallops between sail slides or snaps. Wrinkles parallel to the luff or foot indicate too much. Headsail luffs are normally stressed slightly more than main-sail luffs. Their tension, added to that of the headstay, helps reduce headstay sag under wind pressure. A commonly used indicator of the correct degree of tension is the first appear-ance of a slight crease parallel with the stay or mast while luffing, the theory being that sailing wind pressure will ex-actly smooth it out. The shape of the leech indicates tension in this manner: if it flutters excessively when beating, it is too loose; if it cups or curls, it is too tight. A cup alone adds seriously to drag force. Leech tension is only marginally con-trollable by the crew. Boomed sail leech tension is a result of vang tension, sheet lead, clew position, and sail condition. Many boom-mounted clew fittings have several holes so that the clew cringle can be moved slightly closer to or farther from the boom. If that limited adjustment fails to correct a poor leech, the only recourse is to recut and resew the sail in the leech area. Leeches tend to stretch with time, so it is best to try new sails in the highest clew position possible.

The headsail leech is a bit more controllable since downward tension may be varied by the sheet lead position. The purpose of lead positioning, however, is to equalize tension in the entire sail, not to correct a poor leech. Jib leeches exhibit a greater tendency to flutter than do those of mainsails, probably because of the extra velocity of the wind in the "slot" between sails, and a slight flutter on a hard beat is considered normal. Almost every modern headsail (and many a mainsail) has a light line threaded through the entire hem of its leech, which may be tensioned slightly to control flutter. If a leech line is tight enough to cause cupping, however slight, it is too tight. A few sailors consider a leech line to be a sailmaker's crutch, while most demand it. I'm neutral.

More than cloth and thread, more than devices for splitting air and gathering the wind's subtle power, more, even, than the vessel's wings, or the fancy's, sails are at once the organic and poetic expression of motive, thrust boldly up for wind and vessel to realize one another by. The visible consummation is precisely as perfect as its image. Sails should be beautiful, smooth, still, evenly curved, ideal manifestations of mutuality. Twists, wrinkles, kinks, vibrations, or any discontinuity of this precious interface are just cause for corrective action. If a sail's shape can be redeemed neither by the sailor's devices nor by the sailmaker's arts, it is best to remove its usable parts and consign the remainder to the trash. Tired, shapeless sails are poor performers. An aesthetically pleasing sail is delivering what it is advertising—optimum forward drive.

A bad sail can even disguise a good hull. I once purchased a small fiberglass centerboard cruising sloop from the widow of its second owner, having noticed that its little bilge was filled to the brim with lead in the form of pigs, automobile wheel weights, and various scraps. Obviously the former owner considered her tender, too easily heeled, and had attempted to make her stand up more stiffly. I was surprised, for this design had no reputation for tenderness. Understanding struck when I raised the mainsail the first time. It was a sorry, baggy, shapeless horror that utterly belied the boat's true nature. Since the sail had come with the boat from the factory, I can only surmise that the initial purchaser—inexperienced, disappointed, and reluctant to solicit advice—gave up on sailing and sold the boat to another novice, who was thereby driven to an early grave. Poor quality control had resulted in a too-short bolt rope. When it was replaced, the vessel's bilge was unloaded forever.

Altering Sail Combinations

Alteration of the sail plan—the other response to wind velocity variations—entails expenditures for more sails. The usual "working sails" found on a sloop are a mainsail and a jib that fills most of the "foretriangle," the area between the mast and forestay. This plan is perfectly adequate for driving a modern sailboat in all but the lightest and heaviest airs. Of course, racing sailors, especially those with boats that have a deck and cabin, must seek beyond reasonableness or adequacy in their striving to achieve the maximum performances of which their vessels and resources are capable. The resulting sail inventory can be breathtaking. One well-known 45-foot racing sloop carried an inventory of 23 sails.

The most useful alternate headsail carried aboard cruising types is a *genoa* jib of some kind. Any headstay sail cut for efficiency on all points of sail, and having a minimum measurement between clew and luff significantly greater than the distance between the *tack* (lower, forward corner) of the sail and the base of the mast, is considered a genoa. These are variously designed and sized depending on their intended use. Most will be of slightly lighter material than the "working" jib, since they will be carried in lighter winds, but they must still be heavy enough to hold their shape in a breeze. For racing they are cut very low, often with a deck-sweeping curved foot, or *roach*, to attain still more area. Cruising or casual genoas are often high-cut, which makes them easier to handle and allows the crew to see under them for easier, safer steering.

Although a genoa can usually squeeze a fractional knot or more out of the wind under normal conditions, the payoff for the casual sailor comes in a narrow range of velocities below those that maximize the working jib's efficiency. One boat I knew did well on a beam reach with its working headsail, a *lapper* (clew distance about equal to foretriangle base), down to a velocity of 8 or 7 knots. Below that, she lost her responsive liveliness until her 150 percent genoa (clew distance 1.5

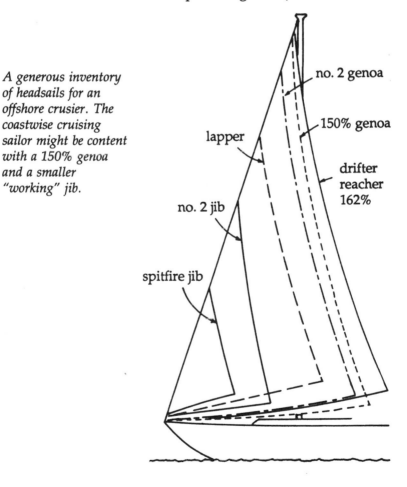

A generous inventory of headsails for an offshore crusier. The coastwise cruising sailor might be content with a 150% genoa and a smaller "working" jib.

no. 2 genoa

150% genoa

drifter
reacher
162%

lapper

no. 2 jib

spitfire jib

times the foretriangle base) was set to work. Then she was back in business until the wind dropped to 3 knots, beyond which, I imagine, nothing could have made much difference. At any rate, she had nothing more exotic to try—no reacher, drifter, or spinnaker—none of which can be carried close-hauled and none of which need be covered in this book.

Reefing

When a sailboat is overpowered by heavy airs, her excessive heeling causes loss of steering control unless the unwanted air is spilled by luffing. Repeated episodes of helm fighting and wind spilling are the boat's sign that she wants less sail. I have learned that sail should be reduced when I first won-

When reefing, reef points are tied together under the foot of the sail using reef knots, which are simply square knots with (as shown) or without a loop taken in the second overhand tuck.

der if it should. Usually, if a large headsail is being flown, a smaller one is substituted. Some skippers reduce their mainsail first, since that sail contributes the most to weather helm. This is accomplished by *reefing*, for which there are several alternative methods.

Traditionally, opposing pairs of short, light lines called reef points were sewn along the sail in two or three rows parallel with the foot. These lines, tied together under the foot, gathered the lower part of the partly lowered sail out of the wind. This method proved cumbersome and exhausting with large sails when underway in reefing conditions. With the popularity of the aluminum boom came the method of rolling the lower part of the sail around the boom. This method's advantages were ease and convenience, but these were outweighed by problems of poor sail shape (including diagonal creases), droopy booms, sticky roller gearing, and limitations on sheet and vang positions.

More recently, the sailing community has adopted an easier version of the old reef point system. Called, variously, "quick," "slab," or "jiffy" reefing, it retains the advantages of both previous methods without presenting any serious disadvantage of its own. The mainsail is momentarily luffed and partially dropped. Then the luff cringle (a grommet sewn into the luff some distance up from the tack) is made fast to a gooseneck hook where the boom joins the mast, and the leech pendant (a line fixed to a corresponding grommet along the leech) is hauled tight and belayed. This creates a new tack and a new clew. The halyard is then hoisted, the sheet is trimmed, and the lower one-quarter to one-third of the sail now resting loosely along the boom is tied, for neatness, with several reefing points. Many vessels are rigged so that another reef can be put in on top of the first, reducing sail area by half or even more.

As fashion dictates and technology allows taller masts and lighter hulls, reefing becomes more frequent. Heavy cruisers laugh at breezes that require light vessels to shorten sail. Reefing the mainsail moves its center of effort downward and forward, ridding the boat of precisely that part of the sail plan most responsible for heeling. On most headings, many boats perform well in breezy conditions without their mainsails, except that they may be harder to tack.

In "quick," "slab," or "jiffy" reefing, one takes up on the topping lift, slacks away on the halyard, trims the sheet hard, hooks the luff cringle on the gooseneck hook, heaves away on the leech pendant, ties the reef points as shown in the previous photograph, eases the sheet, takes up the halyard, slacks the topping lift, and trims the sheet to its proper position.

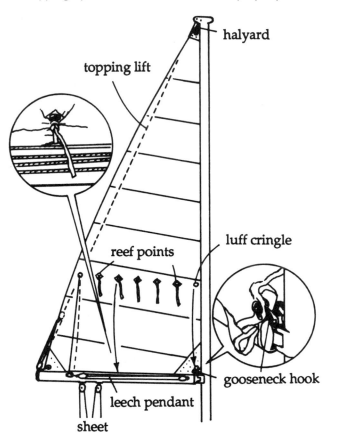

Rope-luffed working jibs equipped with reef points may be reduced effectively, but more often a smaller, heavy-weight storm jib is carried. Extreme sail reduction is the business only of seasoned seamen engaged in grave enterprises. If, while sailing for pleasure, one finds oneself in conditions requiring such tactics as storm jibs and trysails, one has failed, extraordinarily.

Small, open boats normally have no alternative sails with which to increase the area of their sail plans—with the exception of spinnakers for most of the racing classes. Nor do they usually have means to shorten sail, since their working sails seldom have reefing arrangements. When the crew finds the boat is overpowered, the only alternatives are to carry a heavy luff in the main or drop the sail altogether.

Jib or No Jib?

Arguments concerning the relative efficiencies of mainsail and jib will never be entirely settled. The principal one favoring headsails is empirical. A sloop's jib improves the boat's performance to a degree disproportionate to the sails' relative areas. One hypothesis suggests that the part of the sail contributing most to lift and least to drag is the area closest to the luff. That area of the jib is not hidden behind or immersed in the sort of wind turbulence created by a thick mast, since the jib is attached to a mere wire cable. Another suggests that the volume of air gathered by the jib's surface and diverted through the slot between the jib's leech and lee side of the mainsail increases the aerodynamic efficiency of the mainsail by increasing air velocity along its lee side. Both of those elegant arguments have been deeply discounted by some respected sailors, who maintain that much of the gain created by those factors is cancelled by the mainsail's need to be more closely hauled when preceded by a jib, increasing its drag and reducing its lift. You decide.

CHAPTER NINE

Balance, Trim, and Helm

Helm is an essential consideration for both efficiency and comfort. Free the helm and observe the boat's behavior. If she stays on course, the helm is neutral for present conditions. If the bow turns downwind a lee helm is present; if upwind, a weather helm. Slight weather helm is ideal, for if the helm is abandoned the boat slowly rounds up, luffing all sails until directed back on course. By contrast, if a lee helm is abandoned, the boat will fall off the wind and jibe, fall off and jibe, and so forth until she fetches something solid. Keeping course with a lee helm requires constant tiller pressure to leeward as the boat seeks to go off the wind and the helmsman holds her bow up on course. Keeping course with a weather helm requires constant tiller pressure to weather as the boat seeks to round up, and the helmsman forces the bow to stay down where the course is. Weather helm, especially, can be fierce enough to wear out the crew in a short time. Even more unfortunate, dragging the rudder through the water sideways slows a boat significantly.

Helm is controlled by three variables: balance and trim, both of which depend upon the crew, and wind velocity, which is independent of all, some contend, except the whim of Allah. The three are completely interrelated.

Balance expresses the relationship between the sail plan's center of effort and the hull's center of resistance. Each sail's center of effort lies at the approximate center of the sail. When more than one is carried, their average center of effort lies somewhere along the line connecting the individual centers. This is relatively simple to represent graphically. In addition, each hull has a center of lateral (sideways) resistance at the approximate geometric center of its underwater profile. This point is harder to find because the profile's shape is complicated. A means employed in less sophisticated times was to cut the exact shape from a piece of cardboard and find the point at which it balanced, exactly, on a straightedge. That worked surprisingly well. Cruder but equally effective was the practice of drawing a model—or even a completed hull—through the water, attaching and reattaching a line to its side until it drew exactly sideways. That method, which once sufficed for the entire British navy, is probably still used somewhere.

The sail plan is designed and positioned so that a vertical line dropped from its average center of effort falls some proportional distance ahead of the hull's center of lateral resistance. If it falls too far ahead, the boat will have a lee helm in average conditions. If it is too close, or behind, the vessel will carry a disagreeable weather helm. No position is perfect for all conditions, for all angles of heel, or for all points of sail, because a vessel's underwater profile changes with angle of heel, and the center of effort moves forward as sheets are payed out.

It is possible to move a hull's resistance point slightly forward or aft by changing ballast to press one end of the hull deeper into the water. This adds lateral profile area to the ballasted end while reducing it at the other. Depressing the stern and lifting the bow increases the distance between centers, which reduces weather helm. The opposite trim will increase it. Making any but minor fore-and-aft trim adjustment will put the boat "off her lines" as designed, and is probably a poor idea. Interestingly, the center of lateral resistance of a pinned centerboarder can be moved aft by raking the board, a significant helm control device. Also, serious sailors of boats light enough to be sensitive to crew position are very particular about that on various points of sail. Beating requires weight forward, and running, weight aft (but not to the point at which any of the transom is immersed, for that will slow the vessel by dragging water along in her wake).

Small movements can be made in the sail plan's center of effort by raking the mast through adjustment of the rigging. A few boats have mast steps designed with multiple positions, fore and aft, for the mast's base.

Methods for affecting helm while underway consist of altering the shape and size of the sail plan and overtrimming or undertrimming the sails. The latter is the least desirable since it relies on sail inefficiency. Nonetheless, it is handy when conditions change too suddenly to employ the first method. Trimming the jib bare (that is, overtrimming it) to increase drag ahead of the mast, or luffing the mainsail to reduce drag aft, will increase the boat's tendency to turn downwind, the very definition of lee helm. The reverse causes an increase in weather helm. In certain conditions, it is possible to steer a rudderless boat by these convenient changes in helm balance. In the late 1800s, a type of rudderless sailing canoe rigged as a sharpie (cat-rigged ketch) and steered entirely by sail balance and hull trim became popular in the northeastern United States. Windsurfing is another example of balance steering. The mast is tipped forward or aft according to the crew's desire to turn downwind or upwind. It looks like fun, but it isn't easy.

The most effective way to maintain desirable helm is to change the shape and size of the sail plan as conditions change. Reducing the mainsail by reefing, or by substituting a smaller one—or even by dropping it—moves the average center of effort forward to diminish weather helm. Increasing sail area ahead of the mast has the same effect. The opposite actions will reduce lee or increase weather helms.

In light of the foregoing, the cruising sailor begins to appreciate the advantages found with a split rig. Yawls and ketches are more readily balanced. Furling the mainsail is a

quick way to reduce sail, while leaving something aft to balance the jib. Catboats, with their masts far forward, often
immediately behind the stem, allow for tremendous sail area
on the single mast and long boom. Such a large area, fine for
light and medium airs, creates the need for early and repeated
reefing for balance, despite the cat's wide-beam stability.

*A yawl, a ketch, and two catboats. The ketch differs from the yawl in that
the mizzenmast is stepped farther forward—forward of the rudderpost and
usually forward of the helmsman's station. The ketch shown is an Alden
54. The little yawl,* La Mouette, *shows how murky definitions can be: Her
mizzenmast is just forward of the rudderpost, and some might call her a
ketch, but her helmsman's location and the tiny mizzen mark her as a yawl.*

Trim refers here to the hull's lateral, or heeling, trim. (We have already seen the effect on helm of fore-and-aft trim in our discussion of balance.) Trim of dinghies and other small boats can be readily affected by the crew who, in many cases, outweigh the vessel. Crew weight, athletically hiked or trapezed out to weather, can counterbalance strong wind in the sail. Most small centerboarders and multihulls—and many larger vessels, too—are designed to sail best when the hull is upright in the water. The effect of crew weight along the rails on larger vessels, though helpful in racing, is barely discernible. Heeling control is then exercised by presenting a suitable sail plan to the wind in an appropriate way.

The effect of heeling on both comfort and efficiency is very significant and, at the same time, subtle. A hull tipped on its side no longer makes a symmetrical impression in the water. The curvature of the side, digging in to form the shape of the lee side of the impression, contrasts with the flat shape of the impression's weather side created by the boat's bottom. That is one cause of the heeled hull's tendency to turn

A Laser—a tricky and exciting boat to sail—surfs off a wave with spinnaker set and crew hiked out to windward on a trapeze.

to weather. A more powerful inducement to weather helm while heeling occurs because the center of effort in the sails is no longer directly above the center of buoyancy of the hull. When the hull is still flat, with its center of buoyancy on its centerline, the centers of the sails are somewhat to leeward of the center of buoyancy. As the boat heels, the center of buoyancy moves away from the hull centerline, but only a limited distance: it can never reach the rail. This is not true of the center of effort in the sail plan, which can move way beyond the rail during moments of extreme heeling. When this happens, weather helm becomes ferocious, and the tendency to round up, irresistible.

To help visualize the cause and effect of heeling, let us suppose that a little sailboat is being towed by a line fastened to the middle of its mast. All will be well while the mast is kept upright. While the towline's attachment point is somewhere above the deck, the boat is easily steered along in the wake of its power source. Let the crew then heel the boat progressively and the helmsman will experience progressively greater helm, opposite to the direction of heel. Finally, when the towing point gets far enough outside the rail for the mast to act as a lever, the hull, despite extreme rudder angle, turns irresistibly away from the direction of pull. The boat slews off course and is now being drawn sideways by the inattentive towboat skipper, filling the hull with water and capsizing it on the spot.

Excessive helm, if generated by excessive heel, may be eliminated in any of three ways: live ballast to weather; reducing the mainsail; or luffing the mainsail by pointing higher or easing its sheet. It is surprising how precisely one can control the angle of heel simply by playing the mainsheet. This is useful when the wind is flawed with sudden gusts, and essential when near obstructions or in a constricted channel, when one dare not lose steering control.

The subject of helm has turned, without my help, to *wind velocity*, as it invariably must. A boat with too much wind in her sails is overpowered, meaning that she cannot comfortably be steered on a straight course. Wasting wind by starting the sheet to partially luff the mainsail is a short-term stratagem. Balancing the helm in a blow calls for sufficient sail reduction for easy steering. I have mentioned that lowering the center of effort and moving it forward automatically moves it inward also, toward the center of buoyancy. Many

This mainsail carries a partial luff to spill excess wind. Note the battens inserted in sewn pockets in the leech. These long and slender wooden or fiberglass strips stiffen the edge of the sail, giving it a better shape.

boats do well in strong winds under a rather large headsail and a deeply reefed or furled main.

The effect of very light airs on helm is a difficult subject because it is so hard to know exactly what is happening, and why, in such conditions. Sensory input is as faint as the breeze itself. Moreover, the varied reactions of individual boats to drifting conditions make it difficult to generalize. Although most of my sailing has been done in a climate notorious for its light summer airs, I still find myself occasionally confused about the causes of a boat's light air behavior and frustrated in attempts to improve it. Novices seeking clear knowledge of basic principles through experience are well advised to avoid extremely light airs as purposely as heavy ones.

Many boats develop lee helm in light air, because a full main is the maximum sail aft, and the largest headsail aboard is customarily flown to capture what wind there is. Also, any peculiarities of helm induced by current are greatly magnified when the vessel slows to the point where current velocity is a significant percentage of boat speed. Some boats, caught by adverse, ghosting conditions, cannot be steered on certain courses, or even tacked, since the helm is already far alee. Heeling the boat by shifting live ballast to leeward may cancel all or part of an objectionable lee helm by creating the force relationships mentioned a few pages ago. There is another good reason to heel a sailing vessel arbitrarily to leeward in exceedingly light air. When the wind is so light that not even the sails can feel it, this strategy is the only way to get the necessary magical curve into the sails. The force of gravity will hold them out in a more or less proper shape when the wind can't.

In such conditions, the sails should be as still as conditions allow. Crew movements should be minimized, and those that are unavoidable should be made slowly and gently. If only powerboat skippers could suspect the content and intensity of the imprecations showered upon them because of their wakes on very still days! Wind so light that it

cannot be detected except by watching an almost vertical col-
umn of smoke—an incense punk taped to the coaming will
do fine—can be persuaded to ghost a boat along, eerily, if the
sails are well set and trimmed and there is no rolling or pitching motion to shake out of the sails what air they capture.

CHAPTER TEN

A Bit of Rope

Rope is a marvelous invention, probably one of the first. Almost everything a sailor does has something to do with rope, and so at least a few points concerning its handling are in order. How one uses rope becomes, after long experience, a rather personal matter; that's why I can relate only my own approach. There are other approaches, but, for better or for worse, I added the last trick to my repertoire years ago. Apparently, everything I know has grown to include everything I need.

Starting with the only "proper" trick I know, the accompanying drawing shows how to belay to a cleat. Nothing more is ever needed. Something less is needed behind a sheet winch: do not make the tuck.

The way to belay to a cleat.

Round turn

Cross over

Cross over with twist for tuck

Next is the matter of "coiling." My advice is, "Do not." Lines with kinks and twists will not run freely through blocks. They "hang up," causing frustration or worse. Many a racing Snipe has been dumped at the jibe mark because the mainsheet was unexpectedly stopped by a kink. Laid (twisted) line kinks less than braided line, but it, too, will kink with enough provocation. Manufacturers' literature on braided line specifies that conventional round-turn coiling should be avoided. Rather, hanks, if required, should be made up, or flaked, in a figure-eight pattern by passing the line over one's hand in opposing directions. An eight-loop coil requires eight half-twists in the same direction. When the coil is pulled apart by use, the twists remain. Then, recoiling the line in the same direction adds more twists. The figure-eight requires half-twists also, but since each turn is made in

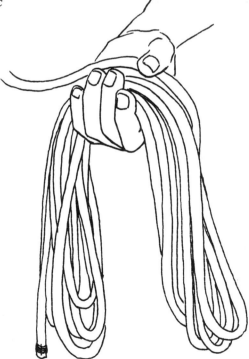

Flaking a braided synthetic line in a figure-eight pattern.

the direction opposite to the one before it, they cancel each other out. Electrical cords and garden hoses work the same way.

Knots are next. Seven of them serve me fully. The few more that have come my way have gone unused.

1. A *slippery reef knot, square knot,* or shoelace bow knot is good for tying the furled mainsail to the boom. One is shown in the photograph on page 64.
2. My stopper knot is a *figure-eight* in the end of the sheets.
3. A *sheet bend,* also known as a *common bend* or *weavers' knot,* ties the ends of lines together and has many other uses.
4. Loops in the ends of my docking lines are made with a *bowline,* an extremely useful knot.
5. An *anchor hitch,* also called a *fisherman's bend,* eliminates chafe in a knot tied to a ring that will have to take a lot of punishment, and also has the advantage of snugging close to whatever you tie to. Using it to attach my dinghy halyard allows the sail to be hoisted higher.
6. Tying a boat temporarily to pilings or tying fenders to lifelines is facilitated by a *clove hitch.* It is best used when some pressure will be kept on the hitch. When there is

A figure-eight knot for keeping a jibsheet on deck (right) *and for restraining a main halyard* (left).

A sheet bend, and one use for it, connecting jibsheets to the clew of a jib.

A bowline being tied, and in use on a temporary docking line.

The anchor hitch and two of its uses, fastening a permanent docking line and a dinghy halyard.

A clove hitch in a bight to secure a dinghy painter to a dock.

A slippery clove hitch on a lifeline supporting a fender.

danger of slipping along a rail or cable, take the first turn toward the side away from the one toward which the slippage is feared. Two turns in that direction are even better.

7. The last is a hitch for which I have no name. I can neither find it in reference works nor recall when I learned it. Perhaps it was as a Boy Scout, and the knot should be called a tent stake hitch, for that is an ideal application. It requires continuous strong tension. After it is tied, it may be slipped along itself to tighten or loosen tension. All the others can be made slippery, so as to be untied by one hand. This one isn't slippery, but can be untied one-handed anyway. I think of it as a "whole hitch" or "jam hitch."

Line ends should be whipped and sewn with a heavy twine, such as waxed nylon. Any other finish fails sooner or later.

I stopped splicing most eyes in lines long ago. If a bow-line will work, I use it. If not, such as at halyard shackles and

A tent stake hitch.

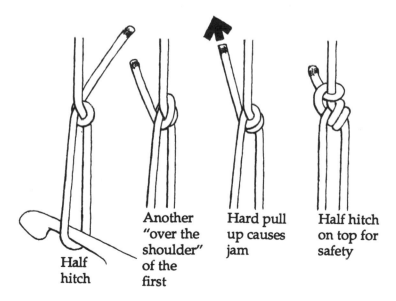

Half hitch

Another "over the shoulder" of the first

Hard pull up causes jam

Half hitch on top for safety

traveler fittings, I sew in two or three tight whips with the doubled line end inside. The sailing fraternity will laugh at such lubberly doings. I don't care. It works without failure and I maintain that in braided line, well-sewn eyes are stronger than spliced ones.

An eye whipped and sewn for a main halyard shackle.

CHAPTER ELEVEN

The Merchandise

This sally into the field of indelicate materialism is no digression. The speed, the ease, the comfort, the pleasure, the degree of success in the learning process, and what is learned, are all functions of the equipment used for learning. Choosing a boat before knowing much about boats is difficult because decisions clouded by uncertainty are the hardest to make. This chapter is meant to lighten the burden by eliminating some traps and illuminating some alternatives, but there is no way that a proper choice can be made for you. Your needs are too personal for any generalizations but your own.

The shapes of our lives seemingly result from our compromises. Add sailboats to the list. Like any land vehicle, each vessel is designed for a certain kind of use under all the conditions expected during that use. Some qualities must be sacrificed in order to realize greater efficiency in the function sought. A few designs fail as learning devices. The relative characteristics of a common design are likely to be objectively known by several persons willing to share their knowledge without much persuasion. An acquisition's foibles may be changed minutely by judicious adjustment of its parts, but what's purchased in the way of basic character is yours until sold.

Naivete can precipitate the error of buying a boat that sails poorly. Such a one will neither teach anything nor give pleasure. There are always a few of them around, passing, after a long time on the market, from one ignorant owner to the next, when the seller either wises up or gives up on sailing. Although many a boat of uncertain breeding sails bewitchingly, one can't be sure until she proves it. Knowledge and feel and time are needed to recognize proof. Better to find one already proven.

To purchase a homemade boat is to gamble. Help the odds by seeking a third opinion from a widely respected expert. Another trap is getting a boat that is inappropriate for the local wind or water, often by virtue of having been imported from someplace it should still be. Deep draft in shallow waters, long overhangs where bad chop is common, large sail plans or tenderness where strong winds are usual—these are ways to acquire frustration even before getting started. For the parsimonious, the trap is invariably baited with a low price.

If your first sailboat is the right one for your ultimate purposes, so much the better. But don't expect her to be. The initial but transitory purpose is to learn, and one will do well, indeed, to find a reasonably priced boat for that purpose which, when its service is ended, can be resold easily. This means acquiring a good boat of a type, class, or model that is, or has been, popular or at least well-respected. To achieve that distinction, it must sail well. Your object, then, is to increase your skill until it equals the boat's potential.

New or old, a boat produced in quantity through the years by a good builder will return good value. One may be found in good condition at a respectable price or, if inexpensive, in such a state that you must pour a lot of yourself into her—which has its own rewards—but do nothing to a popular racing class boat that will destroy her resale value by permanently disqualifying her from competition.

I have observed that the best sailors are small-boat people—or ones who started and stayed that way until they had mastered all a small boat had to teach. There isn't much more. Most small craft are lively teachers. Errors in procedure, technique or judgment are quickly brought to the student's attention, and correct responses are immediately rewarded. With their weight and momentum, large boats ignore many mistakes for a while. They are "forgiving," but that is no true favor to the sincere student. One other point: The smaller the boat, the more easily it can be readied for action and put away afterward, and this results in more frequent use. Also, the crew can "manhandle" a small boat to prevent mistakes from causing expense. An error in judgment resulting in approaching a pier too fast is less costly to both vessel and pier if the crew can fend off effectively before contact.

Something in the way of an open or half-decked dinghy or daysailer between 8 and 18 feet in length, or a catamaran of 14 to 20 feet, is a practical boat to learn on. Successful craft of this size array themselves in a continuum between pleasure and racing class designs. The more popular—and probably the more numerous—are the racing classes, since they enjoy the benefit of frequent press and the enthusiasm of

A dinghy like this can give wonderful sailing.

The Prindle 19, a spritely catamaran that offers lively sailing. It can be sailed off the beach if desired.

The Cape Dory Typhoon is a wonderful daysailer and a great boat to learn in. She's 18¹/2 feet long overall, 13¹/2 feet at the waterline, with a big cockpit for a family and a keel for stability. The boat is no longer being built, but there are plenty of good used ones around.

The O'Day Daysailer is a 17-foot long centerboard boat well suited for kids and for family picnics. Local fleets generate some good racing at yacht clubs around the United States.

In place of the Typhoon, Cape Dory Yachts now manufactures the Typhoon Senior, which is 22 feet 5 inches long overall and 16¹/₂ feet at the waterline. The full keel of the smaller Typhoon is still there (compare with the fin keel of the Soling shown at the front of the book) and there is an outboard motor well and two berths in the small cabin for weekend cruising.

competition. Some racing boats are equipped with sophisticated devices that increase speed by a fractional amount, but
these gadgets detract from early learning and should be dis-
pensed with at first.

Boats designed solely for racing have other characteristics
that may reduce learning efficiency. They are thoroughbreds:
spirited, sporty, demanding, and often wet and uncomfortable. Intended only for the pleasure of winning races, they
are generally splendid sailboats. If a large, active local fleet
exists, it guarantees not only the opportunity to measure a
growing skill against that of experienced skippers sailing
nearly equal equipment (a humbling though profitable activity), but also a ready market when one's best alternative is at
last illuminated by experience.

On the other hand, there's nothing wrong with a little
comfort. I prefer being dry to being damp, and being damp
to being wet, especially in cool weather. I do not fancy a diet

Singlehanding a Laser on a fast run, with centerboard up to reduce resis-
tance. The board is not needed on a run, since there is no sideways compo-
nent of the wind's drag to be resisted.

ot adrenal secretions every time the breeze reaches 20 knots. A daysailer offers excitement of equally high quality but in a quantity more readily savored. Perhaps if I were forty again. . . .

Small sailboats usually have simple sloop or cat rigs. The sloop, in addition to its masted mainsail, carries a jib or foresail on a headstay before the mast. The cat rig, normally used on the smallest boats, features a mast stepped closer to the bow, dispensing with the jib and often with stays as well. With only one sail to trim, sailing is simpler, particularly for one person. With two sails, sailing technique becomes more interesting, but either design will teach basics effectively. A sloop may be sailed with only the mainsail raised. On your first venture, sailing under the main alone may assist your acquaintance with the rudiments of sail trim and steering. Under that arrangement, a sloop is relatively dull and unresponsive because the balance designed into the sail plan with relation to the hull is destroyed. Not until the jib is hoisted and sheeted home does the sloop come to life. A catboat, designed to balance under its large, single sail, will outsail any comparable sloop without a jib.

The three alternative hull styles are: keel monohull; centerboard monohull; or multihull. Each has advantages, and all are suitable for learning. A keel, reaching deep into the water, has a heavy weight, or *ballast,* of lead or iron, affixed to or enclosed within its deepest part. The keel has another function besides leeway resistance. The weight at its end counterbalances the weight of the wind aloft, stiffening the boat against very much heeling. The first few degrees of heel are unresisted except by the shape of the hull, because the weight of the ballast only settles the hull into the water. But when the angle of heel becomes more pronounced, the ballast is lifted sideways, and the greater the angle, the greater the ballast's effect in resisting further heeling. When the boat is heavily burdened by the wind, the keel, held high out to the side, presses downward with nearly all its weight. These boats are relatively comfortable, displaying admirable steadiness, while their momentum, derived from the keel's mass, helps carry them through difficult tacks and imparts the ability to punch through seas that nearly stop lighter craft.

Instead of relying on a keel to resist leeway, a centerboard boat has a movable, boardlike device extending downward through a slot on the hull's centerline. The centerboard can be raised when running or in shallow water by pulling it upward out of its slot (a *daggerboard*) or by pivoting it on a pin into a boxlike well. A few small boats have two boards, one on either side of the centerline, in which case they are called *bilge boards*. And some dinghies and many sailing canoes have boards fastened to both sides, outside the hull, called *leeboards*. Used properly, they all effectively limit leeway, but boards do not contribute to stability or heeling resistance in the slightest measure. In fact, the buoyancy of the wooden board found in the smallest dinghies theoretically detracts from stability. The stabilizing factors for the small, open centerboard boat are the wide, flat shape of its bottom, and the movable ballast, consisting entirely of the very meat and bone of the alert, and preferably nimble, crew.

Any boat may be sailed conservatively by not allowing all the wind to stay in the sail, but to sail a small, unballasted vessel efficiently in a strong breeze requires some agility and an alert hand on the mainsail sheet. The physical demands on the crew vary with each design; on the whole, pleasure-boats behave a bit more sedately, while some of the extreme racing boats require coordinated, highly conditioned athletes concentrating exclusively on the business at hand. Centerboard boats, being somewhat more lively than keelboats, and a little less comfortable, may have a few extra lessons to teach.

One type of monohull that merits special mention is the "board boat"—not much more than an overgrown surfboard with a small footwell, a daggerboard, and an unstayed mast carrying a single lateen sail. They are great fun and might also be called bathing-suit boats, for in sporty conditions they are very wet. But these marvelous cartoppers are not very

The ever-popular Sunfish, not much more than an overgrown surfboard but a lot of fun to sail.

good for more than primary learning purposes, because they sail so easily and with such docility that, unless fleet racing, a beginner can sail all afternoon without realizing the extent of his or her technical poverty. The generous little boats keep the secret well.

The subject of multihulls requires separate attention. In smaller sizes, these boats are designed exclusively for racing. The chief reason for every multihull's existence is the incredible speed it attains in certain conditions. Nearly as much aircraft as watercraft, its performance relies on the contradictory ideals of minimum weight and maximum strength. Every nonfunctional pound slows a multihull significantly. It doesn't take many of them to ruin performance entirely. Yet more strength is needed than is the case with a monohull.

The monohull, as a single unit, easily withstands the twisting and pounding forces of the wind and sea due to its integral strength. A good multihull—composed of two or three widely separated units connected and held together primarily by tensed wire and compressed pipe, with all the thoroughly stressed screws, pins, eyes, and other fittings this implies, and all as thin and light as the designer dared— is an engineering feat inherently weaker than a monohull and stressed more severely by both wind and sea.

A monohull rolls with the blow when a gust of wind slams into the sail. It gathers forward speed in a leisurely manner. A multihull, with its extreme beam (about half its length), and its buoyancy positioned along the outside edges, can't roll in response to the same gust. Instead, the full force of the wind's sudden power creates instant strain throughout the structure, which is transmuted into acceleration. This can be so sudden that crew caught standing may be pitched over the after rail. Obviously the feel of this craft— and the techniques to control it—differ greatly from those of a monohull. Once the basics are past, it teaches somewhat different lessons. In order to obtain a small multihull meeting the criteria of solid popularity and wide respect, one probably must be content with a catamaran. No trimaran that I have heard of has made that grade.

Other comparisons between hull types relate to initial cost, operating expense, transportability, and storage. In each aspect, the unballasted boat has the advantage. Because it can be carried easily on a trailer, this type can be used on any body of water accessible by road. Keelboats are portable, too, but on expensive, specialized trailers, and often only in conjunction with cranes or lifts to transfer them. The larger multihulls must be disassembled or folded for trailering. They, too, require special trailers. The expense of keeping a keelboat in the water or in dry storage far exceeds that of home storage. A small dinghy that can be carried on top of a car is best of all.

A dinghy is a craft small enough to be carried aboard a boat. Moreover, a boat is so small that it can carry nothing larger than a dinghy. A similar relation holds between a boat and a ship: a ship is large enough to carry at least one boat.

In the United States, a dinghy usually is considered to be a rowable craft suitable as a yacht tender, 6 to 12 feet in length, light, undecked, with a board if intended for sailing. The European definition seems to extend to heavier, half-decked vessels twice that length. I suspect that in some areas of the world, any vessel too small to carry one, is one.

Many beginning sailors ignore the subject of dinghy sailing entirely. Perhaps those impelled toward sail by an ambition for blue-water cruising would rather begin with a boat more appropriate to their aspiration. Or sailing may be a means to another end, such as savoring weekend anchorages and galley meals after an exhilarating day in the fresh air. There are many sufficient reasons for beginning the adventure in a small, or not so small, cruising type. My own long-considered advice is to begin with the smallest craft that will satisfy, most modestly, your criteria or passions.

A little cruising boat of 20 to 26 feet on the waterline is an appropriate boat on which to learn to sail. Favor one that has earned respect for its sailing characteristics, which often means a production model made by the hundreds. Well-designed and constructed cruising types are equally seaworthy for local cruising, regardless of their size and materials. They differ in this regard from open boats with exposed bilges.

Small, open boats have built-in or otherwise devised flotation. It is foolish to sail such a craft if it sinks when filled with water, for open boats—especially centerboarders—can be filled fairly easily, given their tendency to capsize when sailed carelessly in a strong wind. No matter. Most are easily flipped back on their bottoms, bailed out, and sailed away. Some needn't even be bailed. An open keelboat carrying ordinary sails is nearly impossible to fill by scooping water in over the coaming because of her positive righting moment and the irresistible weather helm developed by extreme heeling. A few breaking seas could do it, though, if the sailor is foolish enough to be in such a situation. Even in that event, she would not capsize, for the keel's mass would continue to press downward.

The cockpit of a decked boat may get wet in a breaking sea, but with a self-bailing cockpit and a secure cabin, she will not fill with water.

In contrast, a decked boat with a self-bailing cockpit and a cabin secured for sea will not fill with water from above. Significant amounts of water cannot enter the hull as long as the integrity of the hatches and ports is maintained. The cockpit may fill from a sea breaking aboard, but since its sole is higher than the waterline, the sea would drain out through the scuppers. Even when pressed to an extreme angle of heel, or "knocked down," the buoyancy of the air-filled hull keeps all vulnerable openings safely above the new, rotated, waterline.

All cruising vessels have fixed ballast of some sort. Even centerboard cruisers have a short, ballasted keel or internal ballast at their lowest point to ensure positive righting moment in order to stand up again after being knocked down.

It is when water enters from below, through an opening in the bottom, that the ballasted vessel with a deck and cabin is in danger of foundering. Since positive flotation is, traditionally, considered unnecessary in these boats, continuous hull integrity is obviously a matter of special concern.

As the size of a vessel increases, more complicated sail plans become possible, but the principles of hoisting and trimming remain the same no matter how many sails there are. In the final analysis, nothing beats simplicity.

It is sometimes difficult for the beginning sailor to grasp the true relative sizes of cruising types. Briefly, the determinants of size are length at the waterline, displacement (weight), and beam (maximum width). Nothing else really counts—not the height of the mast, or the area of the sails, or the number of berths—especially the number of berths. Compare two vessels of my close acquaintance, both four-berth, keel-centerboard cruisers made of fiberglass-reinforced plastic:

	Mary D	*Music*
Advertised Length	26 ft.	22.6 ft.
Waterline Length	19 ft.	20.25 ft.
Displacement	2000 lb.	3500 lb.

Although not the boats referred to in the text, the Cal 25 (top) and the Express (bottom) show that length is a poor indicator of size. The Express is 27 feet 3 inches long overall and 23 feet 9 inches at the waterline, but her beam, or maximum width, is only 8 feet 1 inch, and she displaces just 2,450 pounds. She is lightly built and fitted out for racing, and is very fast for her length, but her sleeping and living arrangements are spartan. The Cal 25 is 25 feet 3 inches long overall, 22 feet on the waterline, and has a beam of 9 feet. She displaces 4,500 pounds, making her almost twice as heavy as the Express, and some of that added poundage translates as cruising amenities. These boats take the comparison between the Mary D *and the* Music *one step further: When boats are built for different purposes, not even waterline length is a fair indication of relative size.*

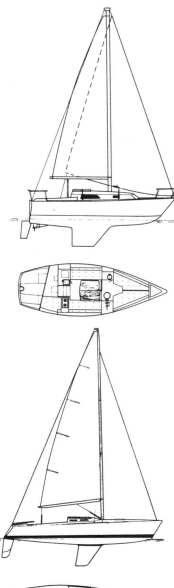

Clearly, the "shorter" is larger than the "longer" vessel by every practical standard and, though she isn't as picturesque, her sailing characteristics are entirely superior. The buyer of the smaller vessel added pipe berths and advertised her for six-berth charter. Fiendish!

All things being proportionate, as a waterline grows linearly, the actual size of a vessel increases cubically. Thus, a doubling in waterline length will increase the vessel's size—weight, sail area, interior space, size and cost of fittings, power needed in the winches, strength required of the rigging, capital investment, inevitable boatyard bills, and everything else—by a factor of eight. For a linear increase of 1.5, the size increase is 3.8, and for only 1.25, nearly 2!

Thinking small makes even more sense when one views small boats in terms of how much fun they are to live with—but not in. It is nice to be able to stand up to pull on one's pants, but that luxury occurs in modern designs only as waterlines approach 24 feet.

It is reasonable to look at a first boat as a piece of merchandise which, after accomplishing a limited objective, will be returned to the market. The romantic overtones associated with sailing should have no part in a boat's selection. In choosing a sailboat to learn with, one should rely on the collective opinion of the sailing fraternity—along with consideration of the guidelines offered above. Sea trials of prospects are of little value because even with considerable experience it is not possible to predict with certainty how a strange vessel, sailed for a short time in one condition of wind and sea, will behave in other conditions. A good boat handles reasonably well in nearly everything, but until nearly everything is experienced with it, one can't know.

CHAPTER TWELVE

A Perspective

Thus far, we have dealt with the basic principles of how to direct the forces operating on one's boat in the most efficient way. There are other considerations, which, not being purely nautical, are absent from the literature. I would wish to leave some of them with any adventurer on the threshold of a sailing career. Some suggestion, phrase, or observation may spell the difference between a long, happy experience for you, or the other kind.

Fear or anxiety commonly accompanies the beginner into any serious enterprise, whether for profit or pleasure. In sailing, nothing could be more natural, for water is a hostile element to us land mammals, and the size and motion of a small boat never allow us to forget its nearness. To cast one-self into the infinitely powerful, impersonal, unpredictable and uncontrollable elements in some frail craft of which one has only a tentative working knowledge is folly undeniable. Not only may one's fears be for the safety of self and vessel, but also for appearing foolish to others if overtaken by situations beyond one's control.

Fear may be suppressed completely beyond conscious-ness. Its frequent manifestation is timidity, which creates a situation wherein little or no learning occurs because there is little or no sailing. Many a sailboat stays on her trailer or in her berth when there's "too much" or even "too little" wind, or because something else needs doing first. The larger the boat, the more common is the last excuse. Alternatively, fitting out may be an operation that spans years, during which the boat is seldom operated except under engine power. The owner may labor faithfully, creating in his sailboat a precise reflection of his talent, great or small, in joinery, engineering, or finishing. When completed, often the boat is sold—generally at a loss—and the process sometimes begins anew.

There are times when it *is* best to stay ashore, but, gratefully, there are more times when it is best to be sailing. A simple hand-held anemometer is an encouraging device by which the beginner may turn an imagined 20-knot wind into a true 10. Guesses, even by seasoned sailors, usually are too high. Eight to 10 knots of wind is ideal for early learning; 3 to 5 knots is the minimum force for good response, depending somewhat on the equipment. A range of 14 to 16 knots affords the best of sailing after one has advanced just a bit. Winds of greater velocity should keep the beginner ashore.

I am convinced that some cases of seasickness or drowsiness are really manifestations of anxiety—as are some displays of shortness of temper, impatience, or other disagreeableness.

Fearfulness can be countered by realistic knowledge gained through experience, and by facing the facts with understanding. A small boat is anything but frail. It survives the normal extremes of wind and sea as a matter of course. Almost invariably, boats can take more punishment than their crews. And, there are simple steps that can be taken to reduce danger: wear a life jacket; put on a wetsuit when a cold-water swim is possible; stay close to home in protected water while building experience; carry and learn the best ways to deploy an effective anchor; watch the sky for trouble; and attempt only maneuvers that seem within your capabilities. These safety measures, most of which apply to sailors of any level of experience, merely amount to ordinary prudence.

As has been explained, some boats can't capsize or fill under any normal conditions. Board boats, which can, are easily righted and sailed away, and that's part of the fun. Those multihulls with floating masts which will not allow them to turn all the way over can be easily righted with a little practice. Some open centerboarders are easy to return and bail out, while some are not so easy. Practice on yours in shallow water. Knowing what to do and how to do it relieves the mind of disquietude.

Excessive heeling—which can easily lead to a fear of capsizing even in boats that can't—is easily controlled, as we have seen, by sail plan adjustment or by paying out the mainsheet until the angles of heel and apprehension subside. If the wind is still too strong, drop a sail or anchor and wait it out.

When one's entire attention is demanded by some pressing need—be it reefing, anchoring, making a repair, extinguishing a fire, pumping, changing a jib, fixing a drink, or finding a sweater—the helm and sheet may be released and temporarily left unattended. Investigate how your boat will behave at such times. Some boats will stay in irons when turned loose, and some will do so with main close-hauled and jib luffing. The helm may need to be lashed amidships. Heaving to—with main close-hauled, jib sheeted to windward, and helm lashed to leeward—is a traditional solution. Experiment. Luffing gently for a while is harmless, but sails —especially headsails—can destroy themselves by flogging in a high wind.

"Being late" is a socially conditioned cause for anxiety. When a boat's progress is stopped by a dying wind, foul tide, head sea, or other unforeseen event, the sailor with no way of getting somewhere else misses meals or other important appointments. The solution lies in planning around the fact that a sailboat is a thrall of the elements. Stay close to port or carry a working engine—the best friend a sailor with something else in mind ever had. A nicer solution is to have no shore commitments.

Columbus, on his second voyage, sailed a fleet of 17 vessels from the Canary Islands to the Antilles. Favored by ideal conditions, he covered 2,500 nautical miles in 21 days. Later in the same trip, working eastward against the foul winds and currents of Cuba's south coast with his three best vessels, he managed only 200 miles in 25 days of hard sailing. One supposes he missed some appointments. A knowing sailor in a hurry to be somewhere else has no business not to be there already. The fortunate sailor is the one who needs to be nowhere else.

Euphoria is the unwillingness or inability to expect trouble. Anticipation avoids trouble, or at least enables one to counter it with well-considered responses, and rarely allows a sense of confidence or well-being to exist unsupported by circumstances. The rational sailor looks and listens for signs of trouble all the time and calculates its probability in every situation. Some, exhibiting a blindness difficult to comprehend, put their vessels, friends, crews, and families into a succession of unpleasant situations. To the detached observer, those that are not dangerous are funny. The pratfall is basic humor, but too many are not funny—particularly for those involved.

Experience, to be valuable, must be accompanied by perception and analysis. The practice of keeping an experience log from the very first forces one to pay attention to what is happening and to think about it afterward. Trying to explain error or an unexpected event is a good way to sharpen the technique of perception. In addition, keeping an accurate log is a good habit for those who intend, someday, to pilot a vessel on a longer cruise.

Spouses require more careful consideration than does sail trim. As a rule, team learning is most efficient. Sailing in mutual enjoyment requires the kind of maturity and regard in which one seeks first for the pleasure of the other. The only true sharing of an experience occurs when each person accurately perceives the reactions of the other, and true camaraderie results when each encourages the other's best possible reaction to the experience. This requires as much attention to each other as to the boat. Then, expansion of knowledge and skill for both parties is inevitable.

It takes only casual observation in the early stages to predict, with some accuracy, the degree of success that will be achieved by a sailing couple.

A word about children: small ones must be rigged to stay aboard, and at least one eye should be kept on them at all times. They should wear life preservers. A sail with children is different from one without, and is wisely approached as such.

It is difficult to choose the place to end a voyage of discovery when much remains undiscovered. We have covered, in just a few pages, material that touches on perhaps 80 percent of what a sailor can know about the subject—the first and most easily assimilated part, the thick of it. For much of the remainder—selection and employment of ground tackle; heavy weather techniques; practical meteorology; the compass; charts; piloting; navigation; rules of the road; hull, rigging, sail, and engine maintenance; safety and first aid; racing rules and tactics; and galleycraft—there is a rich, proliferating literature. The rest, the final 2 percent—the personal, obscure, attenuated, and perhaps the most gratifying—must come as small revelations during the rest of your sailing experience.

Sailing for pleasure is an activity by which many fortunate souls grasp the best there is out of life. If that is your fate, be assured of good company. Certainly, one in tune with wind and water never lacks for challenge—met with knowledge and skills, easily or dearly grasped—nor for beauty, pure and unadorned. But my encouragement is unnecessary. You are already well underway.

Bibliography

If you want to continue your sailing education in the spirit of *Getting Underway*, here are some excellent choices:

Bassett, Frank E., and Smith, Richard A. *Farwell's Rules of the Nautical Road*. Annapolis, MD: Naval Institute Press, 1982.
This is the best Rules of the Road book because it gives the most collision case histories, with court interpretations of the pertinent rules.

Bavier, Bob. *Sailing to Win*. rev. ed. New York: Dodd Mead, 1983.
A classic racing text that will help all sailors improve their techique.

Blewitt, Mary. *Celestial Navigation for Yachtsmen*. Clinton Corners, NY: John de Graff, 1976.
The best book available for the beginner to learn celestial navigation.

Brown, Larry. *Sailing on a Micro-Budget*. Camden, ME: Seven Seas Press, 1985.
The "Small is Beautiful" principle applied to sailing. Brown shows the reader how to get out on the water for less than $5 a day by keeping things simple.

Franzel, David. *Sailing: the Basics*. Camden, ME: International Marine Publishing Company, 1985.
An introductory sailing text with a different angle of approach from Getting Underway.

Henderson, Richard. *Sea Sense*. 2nd ed. Camden, ME: International Marine Publishing Company, 1979.
A classic of seamanship.

———. *Understanding Rigs and Rigging*. Camden, ME: International Marine Publishing Company, 1985.

Jarman, Colin. *The Essential Knot Book*. Camden, ME: International Marine Publishing Company, 1986.

Maloney, Elbert S. *Chapman Piloting, Seamanship, and Small Boat Handling*. 57th ed. New York: Hearst, 1985.
This is the most complete book there is on the facts of small boat seamanship, both sail and power.

Perry, Dave. *Winning in One-Designs*. New York: Dodd Mead, 1984.
A lively complement to Bavier's classic text.

Rousmaniere, John. *The Annapolis Book of Seamanship*. New York: Simon and Schuster, 1983.
Covering much of the same ground as Chapman, admirably, but with a specific focus on sailboats.

———. *A Glossary of Modern Sailing Terms*. New York: Dodd Mead, 1976.

———. *The Sailing Lifestyle: A Guide to Sailing and Cruising for Pleasure*. New York: Simon and Schuster, 1985.
A wealth of practical information on cruising—and a rich sense of its joy.

Royce, Patrick. *Sailing Illustrated*. 8th rev. ed. Newport Beach, CA: Royce Publications, 1986.
"The Sailor's Bible since 1956" in a convenient, tuck-it-in-your-hip-pocket format.

Taylor, Roger. *The Elements of Seamanship*. Camden, ME: International Marine Publishing Company, 1986.
A wise and witty little book. The author's domain is the attitude, the turn of mind, without which sound seamanship is impossible.

Turner, Merle B. *Celestial Navigation for Cruising Yachtsmen*. Centreville, MD: Cornell Maritime Press, 1986.
An excellent text for the navigator who has already mastered the basics or for the studious beginner who wants to learn more than just the basics.

INDEX

Credits

Photography

Page 2, Carol Singer
Pages 4, 57, 59, Story Litchfield
Page 9, courtesy Ralph Naranjo
Page 25, Gail Sleeman
Page 26, Chris Cunningham
Page 36, John Rousmaniere
Page 54, Roger Shope
Page 72 (top), Matthew Walker
Page 72 (bottom), courtesy John G. Alden, Inc.
Page 73, Frank Gordon
Pages 74, 92, courtesy Laser International
Page 90 (top), 91 (top), courtesy Starcraft Sailboat Products
Page 90 (bottom), courtesy Cape Dory Yachts
Page 95, courtesy Alcort Sailboats

Illustrations

Lightning (front of book), Soling (front of book), and
    pages 52, 55, Brad Dellenbaugh
Pages 3, 53, 56, 63, Richard Henderson
Page 66, Jim Sollers
Pages 82, 83, Robert Shetterly
Page 91, courtesy Cape Dory Yachts

Other photos and drawings by the author.